Sales Techniques

Other titles in the Briefcase Books series include:

To learn more about titles in the Briefcase Books series go to **www.briefcasebooks.com**

Sales
Techniques

Bill Brooks

McGraw-Hill

New York Chicago San Francisco Lisbon London
Madrid Mexico City Milan New Delhi San Juan
Seoul Singapore Sydney Toronto

The **McGraw·Hill** Companies

6 7 8 9 0 DOC/DOC 0 9 8 7 6

ISBN 0-07-143001-6

This publication is designed to provide accurate and authoritative information in regard to the subject matter covered. It is sold with the understanding
that neither the author nor the publisher is engaged in rendering legal,
accounting, or other professional service. If legal advice or other expert
assistance is required, the services of a competent professional person
should be sought.
>*—From a Declaration of Principles jointly adopted by a Committee*
>*of the American Bar Association and a Committee of Publishers*

McGraw-Hill books are available at special quantity discounts to use as pre-
miums and sales promotions, or for use in corporate training programs. For
more information, please write to the Director of Special Sales, McGraw-Hill,
2 Penn Plaza, New York, NY 10121-2298. Or contact your local bookstore.

The IMPACT Selling System™ is a trademark of the The Brooks Group. All
rights reserved.

 This book is printed on recycled, acid-free paper containing a minimum of 50% recycled de-inked fiber.

Contents

Preface

Selling is a great profession. However, it is a profession to which many are called and for which few are chosen. What exactly does that mean? Simply this.

There are lots of salespeople. However, there are very few real sales professionals—people who are well compensated, deliver great value to their customers, and experience long-term career success year after year.

This book could help you join the ranks of the great ones. But whether that happens is totally up to you. As you'll discover, sales is a science that, when practiced correctly, becomes an art form. However, not everyone has the talent to be a great artist. Unfortunately, the same is true for sales. Successful selling requires work, study, diligent practice, and endless hours of work.

The unanswered question is simply this: how hard are *you* willing to work? No strategy, tactic, technique, or principle in this book will work unless you work. The challenge is yours. This book is now yours. Now it's time to make its content yours, too.

However, here's the real secret. The things that will make you successful in sales are not for sale. They are already inside of you. Now you must decide whether or not to let them out. That choice is yours.

Why Read This Book?

Whether you are a rookie salesperson or a seasoned professional, there are ideas, concepts, strategies, and tools in this book that will help you propel your career to the next level.

The contents have been honed through over 30 years of sales, sales management, executive sales, training, and sales coaching experience with hundreds of thousands of sales professionals worldwide.

Whether you sell small- or big-ticket items, a product or a service, business-to-business or business-to-consumer, there are hundreds of ideas in this book that can prove to be invaluable to your sales career.

But action is important. Don't take the ideas and just think about them. Take them to the field and apply them. Sales ideas that stay within the pages of a book are worthless. Sales strategies are things to be used daily—to be tested, modified, adapted, or changed as needed in order to make them fit your unique situation.

Overview of the Book

In the first chapter you'll be welcomed to the world of 21st-century selling and learn what real, professional selling is all about. You'll also learn the two biggest mistakes that salespeople make that can derail their careers, followed by the 20 biggest errors to avoid in sales. You'll then learn the seven universal sales rules that can guide your sales career to greater success.

Chapter 2 will reveal the sales profession's most important success secret. You'll also learn how to identify qualified prospects, master the power of understood needs, and learn the big difference between being trusted and simply being liked. You'll read about authority and ability to purchase, urgency, positioning, timing, and the six principles for selling. You will also learn about the powerful IMPACT Selling System™.

Chapter 3 will position you better to understand the power of focus and how to clarify it. You'll learn how to develop your sales philosophy and how to leverage your time, talent, resources, and advantage. You'll also have the opportunity to do an audit of your personal sales talent.

In the next chapter you'll master the power of personal positioning, learn 10 ways to position yourself more effectively with your prospects and customers, and the six ways you can misposition yourself, along with how to avoid those fatal six mistakes. You'll discover how to position yourself as an expert and you'll get tips for dress, style, and image as we discuss the powerful role that your self-image plays in positioning you for success.

The fifth chapter will differentiate between suspects and qualified prospects. It will also delve into niches and segments to better enable you to understand your market. You'll discover powerful qualifying questions, how to maximize your opportunities for success, how to stay organized, the six things you need to know about your prospects, how to organize yourself for success, and much, much more.

Chapter 6 is all about pre-call planning, one of the most overlooked and misunderstood areas in sales. You'll learn how to research your prospects and customers, how to develop internal support, how to review your resources, and how to complete your pre-call checklist. You'll uncover how to mentally and physically prepare yourself for every sales call. You'll learn how to confirm opportunities and how to guarantee that you are ready 100% of the time for every one of your sales presentations.

The next chapter will tell you exactly how to engage customers and prospects face to face. You'll learn how to build trust and rapport and ensure that you will meet every prospect on an equal footing. You'll also learn how to reduce tension, how to be a good guest, and how to move smoothly and easily into your presentation. You'll also learn how to transition to the heart of your presentation in a way that guarantees your prospect will be comfortable with you and mentally prepared to deal with your presentation in the most effective way.

In Chapter 8 you'll learn the power of questions that make the sale. You'll be exposed to the fatal flaw in selling and exactly how to avoid it. You'll read and learn how to be a better listener. You'll also learn the nine things to avoid when asking questions and exact ways to develop questions. You'll also be provided 14 questions you'll be able to ask your prospects no matter what you sell. This chapter will also provide you with the simple, yet most powerful word salespeople anywhere can ever use.

Chapter 9 will tell you precisely how to present your product or service in a way that addresses your prospect's greatest need, want, or desire. You'll finally learn what value really is and how you can deliver it 100% of the time. Among other things, you'll learn how to avoid price issues, how to stress the right benefits, and exactly how and when to present price. You'll also learn exactly how to deflect the age-old "Your price is too high" objection.

You must convince your prospects that your offer is their best option. In Chapter 10 you'll learn exactly how to do this in unique and different ways. It's as simple as this: if your prospects don't believe what you say, they won't buy! You'll learn how to ensure that your prospects will believe and act upon everything you say.

In sales, if you can't finalize transactions, you'll fail. It's really that basic. In Chapter 11 you'll learn powerful, proven, yet simple ways to get to the sale—and exactly how to do it in ways that are not heavy-handed, manipulative, or lacking in integrity.

Sustaining self-motivation and sales momentum is truly an inside job. It has to occur within you. Nobody else can make that happen. The final chapter will reveal to you the 10 most powerful ways that you can stay at the top of your sales game forever. It will tell you how you can be a real sales champion.

Special Features

The idea behind the books in the Briefcase Books series is to give you practical information written in a friendly, person-to-person style. The chapters are relatively short, deal with tactical issues, and include lots of examples. They also feature numerous sidebars designed to give you different types of specific information. Here's a description of the boxes you'll find in this book.

These boxes do just what their name implies: give you tips and tactics for using the ideas in this book to intelligently manage the sales process.

These boxes provide warnings for where things could go wrong when you're planning and dealing with sales situations.

These boxes give you how-to and insider hints for techniques professionals use to create the mutually beneficial relationships that lead to sales success.

Every subject has some special jargon, including this one dealing with sales techniques. These boxes provide definitions of these terms.

It's always useful to have examples that show how the principles in the book are applied. These boxes provide descriptions of sales principles in action.

This icon identifies boxes where you'll find specific procedures you can follow to take advantage of the book's advice.

How can you make sure you won't make a mistake when you're dealing with a prospect? You can't, but these boxes will give you practical advice on how to minimize the possibility of an error.

Acknowledgments

This book would not have been possible without the help of some very special people. Clearly, I have learned a lot more from my clients than I ever taught them, and their confidence and belief in my ideas over the years have made my life much more fulfilled.

Bonnie Joyce, my long-time assistant, made this book possible. Revision upon revision went her way without one word of complaint. She's a real champion.

My wife, Nancy, learned to live with an already hectic schedule that got worse as I developed this manuscript. Our son Will's efforts are also deeply appreciated. He now sees the values of a degree in English!

I'd also like to thank you, the reader. It's your expectation for quality that drives me. I hope we have exceeded that expectation.

About the Author

Bill Brooks is universally regarded as one of the most authoritative and respected sales writers in the world. A former award-winning sales professional, he is CEO of The Brooks Group, a full-service sales training and sales management education firm based in Greensboro, North Carolina. In great demand as a speaker, he is a member of the Speaker Hall of Fame. He is also a Certified Management Consultant. Mr. Brooks is the author of 11 other books on sales, sales management, and related peak performance topics. He can be reached at 800 633-7762 or via e-mail at bill@thebrooksgroup.com. He can also be found on the Web at **www.thebrooksgroup.com**.

Sales Techniques

21st Century Selling

The final decade of the 20th century saw more changes in the world of selling than the previous 90 years of the century. And this century's changes promise to dwarf those changes in speed, magnitude, and velocity.

So, congratulations! You are about to jump on board a fast-moving train. However, no matter what your level of sales experience, this book will deal with the newest, most up-to-date ideas and proven strategies. Welcome and all aboard!

What Is Sales All About?

Professional selling is all about getting in front of the right people with the right message at the most opportune time. It's all about how you position yourself and your organization, prospect for business, properly plan your presentations, build trust, and uncover the right set of answers that your prospects are looking for. It's about how you make your answers or solutions available to your prospects under the conditions and terms that they are most interested in. It's creating compelling

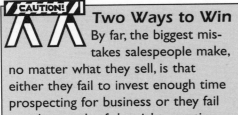

Two Ways to Win
By far, the biggest mistakes salespeople make, no matter what they sell, is that either they fail to invest enough time prospecting for business or they fail to ask enough of the right questions when they do get in front of a qualified prospect.

value for your product and maximizing margin. It's then servicing your new accounts in order to exceed their expectations, sell them more, and use them as referral sources. That's sales. And it's that simple. But not so easy.

The 20 Biggest Errors in Selling

Selling may require a slightly different approach based on the product or service you're selling, the type of prospects, and the nature of the sales cycle or process that is required to sell it.

However, regardless of what you're selling, there are 20 errors that could prove to be fatal to you:

1. Talking too much and listening too little
2. Not asking enough questions
3. Too little pre-call planning
4. Inconsistent or insufficient prospecting
5. Quoting price too soon
6. Not creating value
7. Presenting too many features
8. Giving a presentation that doesn't address the issues the prospect wanted to address
9. Raising objections yourself by talking too much
10. Not listening
11. Failing to provide proof of other, happy customers
12. Asking leading questions
13. Using tie-down questions (e.g., "If I could show you a way to save money you'd be interested, wouldn't you?")
14. Memorizing canned closing techniques or ways to overcome objections
15. Not having a flexible personality
16. Dropping your price too soon

17. Making claims that can't be backed up by facts
18. Underdelivering on promises
19. Not revealing all the facts
20. Failing to ask for the order

Put Yourself in a Position to Win
Knowing what *not* to do can be as valuable as knowing exactly what you should do. Smart salespeople avoid losing a sale as aggressively as they work to make the sale. Don't be your own worst enemy. Know the biggest errors—and then avoid them!

The Seven Universal Rules for Sales Success

Now that we've listed the 20 biggest mistakes, let's talk about how to avoid making them. In order to avoid them all, there are just seven universal rules that you need to follow. These universal rules will serve you well no matter what you sell or to whom you sell it.

These universal sales rules are based on a series of principles that have proven successful with hundreds of thousands of salespeople worldwide. Here are the rules:

1. Proper positioning, prospecting, and pre-call planning will guarantee that you will be in front of the right people with the right message at the most appropriate time.
2. Building trust with the buyer is based on the proper approach and not dominating the conversation.
3. Professional selling is based on asking enough of the right questions in the right way and not determining or presenting any solution until you have discovered:
   - What they'll buy
   - When they'll buy
   - How they'll buy
   - Under what conditions they'll buy
4. Properly presenting your solution based on the conditions, terms, and parameters under which your prospect will buy is the essence of the successful sale.
5. People expect salespeople to make claims for their product

How Full Is Your Toolbox?
The salesperson's best tools are the energy to prospect, the interest to research prospects, and the patience to learn about the prospect before the face-to-face sale ever starts.

or service. They are impressed, however, when someone else does it or if they are able to experience claims themselves.

6. No sale is ever made unless you ask someone to buy your product.
7. The real work begins after your first sale.

The Universal Rules in Detail

Let's take a look at each of these principles in some detail.

Principle 1: Proper positioning, prospecting, and pre-call planning will guarantee that you will be in front of the right people with the right message at the most appropriate time.

Top sales professionals invest a lot of time in everything that occurs prior to the sale. Amateurs and marginally performing salespeople tend to wait for prospects to find them and then subsequently are ill-prepared to deal with prospects in any type of intelligent, well-informed way. For example, 21st-century sales pros know and understand the power of networking, the Internet, direct marketing, oriented e-mail campaigns (as distinct from spam), and even seminars and authorship to prospect for business. They understand the difference between *pull* prospecting and *push* prospecting.

Successful salespeople know that pull prospecting tends to posi-

Positioning The relative ranking or perception that prospects and customers have of you, your product, and/or your organization relative to your competition.

Prospecting The proactive steps taken to identify, isolate, and get in front of qualified prospects.

Pre-call planning The research, data gathering, and preparation that you must make in order to be totally prepared for a sales presentation.

tion them better in the marketplace as true, winning sales professionals. In the final analysis, people want to do business with you if you are a busy, highly sought-after professional far more than if you appear to be a desperate, hungry, aggressive salesperson seeking your next dollar.

Key Term

Pull prospecting Attracting prospects through a broad-based process that could include such methods as authorship, networking, and gaining industry specific celebrity status.

Push prospecting Contacting prospects one at a time, individually, proactively, through such methods as cold calling or phone solicitation.

Pre-call planning is perhaps the most overlooked, yet essential selling skill you can master. You need to gather essential information before you ever attempt to get in front of anyone, anywhere. Pull prospecting allows you the opportunity to invest more time in this process because you can invest time in the most valuable prospects—those who respond to you. If you are simply running up and down the street asking people to buy, you have no time to invest in learning about prospects and their organizations before you ever get in front of them.

Knowledge Sells

Mistake Proofing

It is far better to position yourself as a business advisor, strategic partner, industry expert, or product-specific guru than to position yourself as a salesperson. Unfortunately, salespeople are just not positioned nearly as well in the marketplace as the others are.

Principle 2. Building trust with the buyer is based on the proper approach and not dominating the conversation.

In professional selling, building trust is far more important than just being liked. A fatal flaw for salespeople occurs when they believe that they need to "sell themselves to the prospect." This is not correct: it is "old school" selling and leads salespeople to eventually overselling themselves.

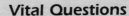

Vital Questions

Ideally, you should research the following issues before you ever get in front of any prospect:

- Who will I be competing against?
- What questions is the prospect likely to ask me?
- What is the formal and informal structure of the prospect's organization?
- Is the person I'm calling on a decision maker or influencer?
- How can I develop internal advocacy?
- What is the biggest single problem I can help the prospect solve?
- How far along is the prospect in the buying process?

You need to understand and remember that being trusted is truly more valuable than being liked when selling. Also, once you're trusted, it generally follows that you'll be liked. You need to avoid seeking approval.

This doesn't, however, mean that you should be rude, offensive, or abrasive. But it also doesn't mean that you need to be overly aggressive, dominate the conversation, or be too friendly, too soon, either.

Aim to Be Trusted, Not Liked

If you build trust, you're in a better position to sell value. If you seek to be liked, you're only going to be able to sell price. Buyer trust means that the prospect has the belief, confidence, and full expectation that you, the salesperson, are a person of integrity and that you and your organization will deliver all that you promise.

Principle 3. Professional selling is based on asking enough of the right questions in the right way and not determining or presenting any solution until you have discovered:

- What they'll buy
- When they'll buy
- How they'll buy
- Under what conditions they'll buy

To excel in sales, you'll need to excel at asking the right questions and then concentrate on listening to the answers, recording those answers both in writing and mentally, and then prescribing the exact solution that your prospect is seeking based on those answers.

> ### Don't Overwhelm
> Good salespeople don't dominate the conversation. They also don't come across as too aggressive. They don't offer *unsolicited* small talk. If the prospect wants to talk, let him or her talk. If not, simply tell the prospect why you're there and what you'd like to accomplish on that call.

This is perhaps the most fundamentally overlooked secret to successful, smart selling. The biggest error that you will need to avoid is the tendency to start explaining how your product or service works, looks, functions, or performs without knowing exactly *how* the prospect wants it to work, look, function, or perform.

If you neglect universal sales rule 3, you'll lose far more sales than you'll ever make. You cannot presume, ever, that you know exactly, precisely, and accurately how to present your product or service unless you know exactly how your prospect wants to see it! And the only way to do that is to ask the right questions.

> ### Understand First
> Most salespeople start to provide solutions before they've learned about the situation!
> To guarantee that you always ask your prospects enough of the right questions in the right way, never go on a sales call without prepared questions that allow the prospect to answer these questions. Then never, ever begin telling, selling, demonstrating, or discussing your product or service until you've got precise and exact answers to your four questions—what, when, how, and under what conditions.

Principle 4. Properly presenting your solution based on the conditions, terms, and parameters under which your prospect will buy is the essence of a successful sale.

Smart salespeople understand that there's a big difference between badly outdated price and demonstration selling and 21st-century application-based selling. You will, indeed, become

Application-based selling Presenting the product or service in the context of precisely how it can be applied to solve your prospect's biggest problem, agitation, or difficulty or to address a solution your prospect is seeking. This is in contrast with focusing on features, benefits, price, or design. Your prospects are looking for answers. Application-based selling is the essence of professional selling.

a real sales master once you understand this truth.

People can focus on only one thing at a time. And where you place that singular focus can have a lot to do with your sales success. Let's take a look at the four potential areas where you can focus:

1. yourself
2. your product or service
3. your organization
4. the prospect

The only way to focus correctly is to have a deep-seated, 100% total commitment to building and sustaining a focus that's

How Do You Focus?

Consider the following three situations. How do you focus appropriately?

You've had a bad morning and you're in a miserable mood. Everything has gone wrong. Your child is sick, your car needs repairs, and the bills are due. Your focus has been on yourself and how you can deal with all of these problems. However, you have a sales call at 1:00 p.m. How do you suddenly and easily shift gears?

You've had quality, service, and delivery glitches with your product. You're concerned that it may not function, yet you've just gotten an upgrade announcement and have to learn 32 pages of new, technical information. Is your focus on whether the upgrade will work? You're going out on a sales call. How do you prepare to focus?

You just heard that your company may be sold and you don't know if the sale will affect your future. Where is your focus? You now have to go to a critical sales presentation and put on a great show. How do you shift your focus?

solely on your prospects and customers. You must be able to compartmentalize your life and your thinking so you can commit every phase of your presentation to the one, single thing that drives sales success—a singular focus on your prospects and customers. Period.

Principle 5. People expect you to make claims for your product or service. They are impressed, however, when someone else does it or if they are able to experience claims themselves.

You have something to gain if you make a sale. You know that and so does your prospect. Unfortunately, lots of people have dealt with salespeople who stretched the truth and they remember that. Also, some have become jaded by oversell.

The only way for you to go is to be in a position to offer your prospects the opportunity to talk with satisfied customers, to read strong testimonials from them, or to actually experience the value of your product or service themselves.

It's essential to select your testimonials with great care. You need to be sure that they are strong and describe you and your product or service and organization in the most positive and powerful ways possible. That's why you need to solicit these letters and comments from totally pleased and highly satisfied customers.

Another method would be to ask your customers to agree to be on a list you compile for prospects to contact if they choose to do so. This is another proven, powerful way to involve your prospects with super-satisfied customers who can verify your claims.

Developing Testimonials

To get satisfied customers to be willing to place their comments in writing, here's what you must do:
1. Convert prospects to customers.
2. Service and deliver in ways that exceed expectations.
3. Follow up to be sure your customers receive what you sold them.
4. Ask them for a strong reference.
5. Thank them and continue to service their accounts.

Get Customers to Help You Sell

To get customers to agree to be on a list of satisfied cus-
tomers for prospects to contact, you should take the follow-
ing steps:
- Solicit their involvement.
- Tell them that you will rotate them off the list regularly.
- Ask them to provide their name, address, phone, and e-mail or fax.
- List the type of service you've provided to them.
- Ensure them that you will phone them if you expect that a prospect may contact them.
- Send them a thank-you note or small gift whenever they talk with a prospect.

Tests and trials of your product or service allow your prospects to actually experience your claims and are valuable. However, if you're going to provide the opportunity for some sort of limited experience with your product or service, be totally sure that you establish the parameters that define a successful trial exactly and that you fully expect your prospects to buy your product or service based upon a successful outcome of the trial.

Principle 6. No sale is ever made unless you ask someone to buy your product.

In the final analysis, your success in sales is determined by how much of your products or services you can be responsible for someone buying. That means being assertive enough to ask someone to buy what you're selling.

How to Do Trials Without Errors

To have a successful trial of your product or service, you need to clarify exactly what a successful outcome is. In order to do that, you need to:
1. Define what your prospect is looking for and what the outcomes of the test should be.
2. Establish a method for evaluating the results objectively and for implementing your product or service properly.
3. Set the criteria that the trial results must meet for you to assume that your prospect is pleased and ready to buy.

It's not unusual for salespeople to get caught up in the process and never ask anyone to buy. You must avoid that at all costs. The real puzzle is to learn why so many salespeople go through the hard work of prospecting, getting in front of a prospect, and making a great presentation—and then fail to ask the prospect to buy. You need to avoid that at all costs!

Closing

Closing sales is a consequence of what has happened earlier in the sale. It's not something salespeople build toward. However, if you don't ask prospects to buy, most will never buy on their own. So you must urge them to take action. Most people need help in making decisions, so you should suggest the steps they need to take in order to make the decision to buy your product or service.

Smart Managing

Part of the foolishness of unprofessional selling is to teach someone the "20 power closes" or "10 changed scripts to follow to overcome objections." The real truth is that you are far better off learning one or two ways to close sales or deal with issues and using them correctly than having a whole host of manipulative tricks that you're hesitant to use and that probably won't work, anyway.

Remember this: if you don't ask your prospect to do something, nothing will happen! And then, unfortunately, you've become a professional host, a visitor, or a tour guide. And you're none of those. You're a professional salesperson.

Simplicity Sells

Most successful salespeople use some form of the assumptive close. They don't use manipulating maneuvers. Old school selling suggests that you learn "the puppy dog close," "four-square close," "Ben Franklin close," "impending event close," etc. The truth is that it is best to act as if the prospect has agreed to buy. Simply say or ask some form of the following:

• Can we go ahead and get started?
• Let me show you how we can move ahead.
• Shall we handle the paperwork now?

Mistake Proofing

Principle 7. The real work begins after your first sale.

Professional salespeople know that servicing accounts, exceeding expectations, anticipating problems, and being available instantly are all part of the sale—even though these things occur after the sale is made. Hit-and-run salespeople don't understand this at all. Their philosophy is to make the sale at any cost, promise whatever is necessary to get the sale, and then do all in their power to avoid having to deal with their new customer again.

You need to understand that earning the customer is the hard work. Your job is to convert prospects into customers and then do all in your power to sell them more when they legitimately need something you have and to keep them more than totally pleased. So pleased that they will readily refer you to more prospects like them and agree to serve as sources for top-flight testimonials to help your sales effort.

However, in order to earn this right, you'll need to establish a long-term relationship based on superior service, total integrity,

A True Story

Barry bought a new office condominium. After renting for almost 15 years, he decided that it made more sense to own a building and rent offices to himself, with his company paying him. It seemed like a good idea. And it was.

Unfortunately, Barry dealt with Robert and Richard. When he started to do the construction, Barry found a problem. Apparently, the office next to his had purchased 1200 extra square feet that hadn't shown up on the final blueprint.

Robert couldn't be found and Richard denied any wrongdoing. So did the developer and the architect. Barry ended up having to pay extra rent in his old facility since construction slowed by two months, his new offices were 1200 square feet smaller than anticipated, and he's still looking for Robert and Richard to help him!

Would you consider Robert and Richard professional salespeople or commission-seeking opportunists? How quickly will Barry refer either of them? Will he purchase more property from them? How about the developer and architect?

commitment to delivering what you promised, and consistently treating your new customers as your most valuable prospects—because that's what they are.

Many salespeople do not seem to understand this universal rule or maybe they just do not believe it. It's really the difference between sales as *transactions* and sales as *relationships.* Making a sale is the first step in forming a relationship. Future sales to any customer depend to at least some extent on how you handle the first sale.

One recommendation is to make a follow-up call within a short time after the sale. It's a good way to find out if your customer has any questions or problems—before he or she worries or gets upset or complains to others. You may also learn something about the product or service that will help you sell. After more time passes, it might be smart to send a personal thank-you note. Such simple steps help build a relationship by going above and beyond the sale as a transaction.

Sales as a Profession and Where You Fit In

Sales is a profession. It's far more than just a job. And, as a profession, it provides you the opportunity for significant income and exceptional prestige if you are a top performer. It requires specialized skills and training for superior performance. It also allows you to bring great value to your customers.

However, in order for you to be able to get the most out of sales as a profession, you'll need to believe in what you do and how you do it. And you must believe that the skills and strategies you master are credible, professional, and totally honorable.

Sell with Integrity

To ensure that you feel good about what you do and how you do it, it's essential that the skills you learn, assimilate, and apply be consistent with your value system. Applying old school, manipulative techniques flies in the face of the way most 21st-century people want to feel about themselves and creates a situation where you don't believe in what you do or feel good about it. This is demotivating. Avoid it at all costs.

Once you've employed a process that is totally focused on the customer or the prospect, is based on sound and honorable principles, and allows you to feel good about what you do and how you do it, you're on your way to being a sales professional. Then you'll become a top performer in one of the world's most lucrative and valuable professions.

Checklist for Chapter 1

❏ Professional selling is all about getting in front of the right people with the right message at the most opportune time.

❏ Selling is how you position yourself and your organization, prospect for business, properly plan your presentations, build trust, and uncover the right set of answers that your prospects are looking for and then how you make your answers or solutions available to them under the conditions and terms under which they are most interested in buying them.

❏ Regardless of what you're selling, there are 20 errors that could prove to be fatal to you.

❏ To avoid errors in selling, there are seven universal rules to follow, based on a series of principles that have proven successful.

❏ Sales is a profession, not just a job. It provides the opportunity for significant income and exceptional prestige if you are a top performer and it requires specialized skills and training for superior performance.

❏ As a profession, selling is based on sound ethics and standards. Help the profession and yourself by following those standards.

Professional Selling: The Insider Secrets

What would it mean to you and your sales career if you learned the single most essential, critical, and fundamental secret behind selling successfully? What if you could master the one, simple truth that over 95% of all salespeople in the world have no idea even exists, let alone have any clue about how to implement?

First, you would undoubtedly slice years off your learning curve. Second, you would be equipped with a unique insight that could propel your sales career instantly.

But shockingly, you would also be handed a huge burden. You're probably asking yourself, "Burden? How could something so valuable prove to be any kind of a burden?" That burden is the responsibility that such a powerful insight can place on you. Because to know a universal success secret and not implement it would be tantamount to career suicide—it could derail your career forever. That's a big burden! Failing at anything when you know precisely how to be successful at it is unacceptable.

The good news is that this insight, along with hundreds of

selling secrets, will be revealed in great detail throughout the remaining chapters of this book. But, for now, let's settle for a quick look at this career-changing truth.

Selling's Biggest Success Secret Revealed

The secret to selling is to be *in front of qualified prospects when they're ready to buy, not when you need to make a sale.*

Are you surprised by that simple, yet profound principle? To understand what's behind this truth, it's important to examine it carefully. Probably the quickest way to do that is to break it into its three fundamental parts. You need to:

1. be in front of qualified prospects ...
2. when they're ready to buy ...
3. not when you need to make a sale!

The Five Characteristics of Qualified Prospects

Have you ever tried to sell your product or service to someone who wasn't qualified to buy it? Being "qualified" means the prospects have five critical characteristics:

1. They have a need for what you sell and are aware of it.
2. They have both the authority and the ability to pay you for it.
3. They have a relative sense of urgency about the decision.
4. They have a significant level of trust in you and your organization.
5. They are willing to listen to you.

Your best prospects will have all five of these characteristics at the same time. Those who have fewer will become progressively less qualified as more of the characteristics disappear. For example, a prospect with four of the five is better than one with just three. Three is better than two and two is better than having only one of the characteristics. The secret, though, is to invest most of your time with those that have all five.

The biggest challenge you'll face is to avoid settling for

Don't Waste Your Time

Smart salespeople don't waste a lot of time in front of prospects who don't have all of the qualifying characteristics. What would you think if a person called you and said, "I really like what you have. Come and see me today"? Would you be excited about already having made a sale? Or would you ask the person a few questions—like the following:

- How did you find out about us?
- What are you looking for from a product like ours?
- What kind of a time frame are you working with?
- How much do you know about our organization?

When you have answers to these questions and it makes sense, establish a time for an appointment.

---

being in front of prospects who only possess characteristic #5: they are simply willing to listen to you. One of the best ways to eliminate this error is to avoid falling prey to the temptation to pile up sales calls simply for the sake of hollow opportunities, to mistakenly believe that sales is a "numbers game." It is not— and successful salespeople know better.

The Power of an Understood Need

You must be in front of prospects who have a need and are aware of it. Just ask any experienced salesperson how successful he or she has been at trying to "create" a need and you will learn how fruitless that effort can be. By the same token, selling bottled water at every rest stop in the desert, blood in an emergency room, or portable generators during a power outage are quite different stories—and much better ones, too.

The Beauty of Both the Authority and the Ability to Purchase

Have you ever tried to sell your product or service to someone who had all the authority and yet no ability to pay for it? Or someone who had lots of ability but no authority? The result is the same: no sale. The only thing that's worse is to be in front of someone who has neither authority nor ability.

However, when you are in front of someone with both the

responsibility to purchase and the authority to do so, you are in the right zone. That's where your efforts can really pay off.

The Urgency Factor

There is a great thing about urgency: it forces prospects into doing things that they may have viewed as being difficult, complex, overwhelming, or demanding. There is, however, another truth about urgency: a salesperson can't force any false sense of urgency on a prospect. Today's buyers are too sophisticated for the old school sales ploy that said, "Create a sense of urgency"—like "The price goes up tomorrow" or "This is the last one we'll ever have." Urgency must be legitimate, identified, owned by the prospect and a true reality from their own, personal perspective, not yours.

You Can't Create Something That's Not There

A sense of urgency must be legitimately felt by your prospect. You cannot artificially create it. That's manipulation. And manipulation isn't selling. It's pure deceit and a dishonest misinterpretation of the truth. Old school selling went something like this, for example: "If you can't buy today, our factory will never make one of these like this ever again." What type of reaction do you think this type of artificial ploy would elicit in today's market, where every customer has a host of suppliers to choose from?

Trust vs. Like

Is it more important to be liked or to be trusted? It's not even a contest. Trust is essential. In fact, in today's competitive marketplace, it may be the single most important factor. Being trusted leads to selling value. Being liked merely leads to selling price. And you can bet on it, value is a far better selling tool than price—100% of the time. And it's a lot more profitable, too.

It's All About Their Time Frame, Not Yours

Getting in front of a qualified prospect could be the trickiest part of selling. However, the second part of that formula is to be in front of them when they're ready to buy. The truth is that people buy according to their time frame, not yours. Whether it is a corporate buying cycle, a budgeting calendar, an individual consumer's spendable cash from a financial windfall, the time when equipment becomes unusable or replaceable, or any time frame that drives the decision, the reality is that prospects will buy when they're ready.

Some people might argue that you should push prospects into a decision. But the real truth is that pushy salespeople lose far more sales than they ever make.

This timing issue has a lot of hidden meanings for you. It means that you

> ### War of Wills: You Lose
>
> When a prospect and salesperson engage in a war of wills, the salesperson will always lose. For example, when a salesperson starts to dictate terms, conditions, requirements, or limitations, he or she will lose every time. The reason? Customers have choices. The law of supply and demand is on the customer's side, working against you.

must do a lot of homework so you better understand the dynamics related to purchasing cycles and time frames. You will have only marginal success if you have a limited understanding of a prospect's time frame as it relates to seasonality, release of budgets, new product launches, or any of the other scores of variables that could influence the timing of purchases.

Know the Buying Cycle

If you want to have a great sales month, first analyze the length of your sales cycle and the number of qualified prospects you will need to have at that precise point in time and then factor that data into what that will mean to you at specific times in the future. You need to do this every single month. You will then have consistent sales months sequentially. Fail to do this and you will never get any traction. Do it now and you will have success every month.

If you're having a bad sales month now, you likely caused the problem two, three, or four months ago, depending on your average sales cycle. It's as simple as that. So, to avoid problems in the future, start now.

It's Not About When You Need to Make a Sale

One of the most curious dynamics of selling is the role that panic plays in a salesperson's performance. Yes. Pure, outright panic!

Based on your pay plan, it may not be uncommon for you to have too little money left and too many bills due on the last day of the month. The result? You're not able to make car or mortgage payments, pay insurance bills, buy groceries and gas for your car. So you need to make a sale.

But prospects don't care about your problems. And, in the final analysis, you've created this set of difficulties yourself. You've failed to be in front of enough qualified prospects when they were ready to buy. So don't point the finger at others, including your prospects. Go look in the mirror.

TRICKS OF THE TRADE

Who's in Control?

Never forget: prospects buy for their reasons and according to their time schedule for purchase. They don't buy for your reasons or when you need to make a sale.

The trick is to find out what they want to buy, when they want to buy it, why they will buy, and under what conditions they will buy and then provide it to them on those terms and within their time frame. The key is to get all of this information from the prospect and then package your solution in those terms. Your challenge is to ask the right questions to get the answers on how to present your solution.

It's really that simple. Don't make it any more difficult.

The Two Most Essential Components of Professional Selling

The two most essential components for closing a sale are *positioning* and *timing*. It's ironic that these two components are things that you may not even associate with selling. As a result, they are far too often overlooked and vastly undervalued. But once you have understood and mastered them, everything else in sales becomes easier for you.

Positioning

This is a critical strategic advantage that few sales-people understand. It's a fundamental truth of life that perception is reality. And the perception most people have of salespeople isn't good. Therefore, it's critical that you invest lots of time, effort, and energy and then have the common sense to create a persona that keeps prospects from seeing you solely as a salesperson. Ask 100 people on the street to respond to the word "salesperson"

What Is Positioning All About?

Smart Managing

As I mentioned in Chapter 1, positioning is the relative ranking or perception that prospects and customers have of you, your product, and/or your organization relative to your competition. It's the way they view you and your organization. Are you considered equal to, better than, inferior to, or somewhat like your competitors? Are you seen as the high-end, expensive source or are you seen as the bargain-basement provider? Are you seen as the Rolls-Royce or the Chevrolet of your market? Either one is fine. However, you need to decide where you need to be.

and there is a great chance that their responses will not be good.

Your personal positioning is one thing you could easily overlook as you build your sales career, but it could be the most valuable and essential tool in your kit. Smart salespeople know the value of personal positioning and use it as a strategic advantage.

Add Value

Mistake Proofing

People pay attention to people whom they perceive as having something important to say to them. Therefore, you need to be seen as someone who brings value to the relationship. You need to position yourself correctly.

Great salespeople position themselves as something other than salespeople. They position themselves as industry experts, advisors, advocates, authors, coaches, consultants, unpaid team members, or one-of-a-kind assets. When they do that, they are seen as valuable people contributing vital and essential expertise. Prospects will often do business with them to gain access to their expertise. Their product or service just happens to go along with it.

Sarah vs. June

Sarah and June both sell office supplies, but they're quite different.

Sarah believes that cold-calling is the only way to find new prospects and it has been her primary strategy for 10 years. She literally dials for dollars all day long, sometimes making 50-75 calls a day. She still even goes door to door in industrial and other commercial areas. She has been selling for the same employer for six years and has sold similar products for four years before that.

June is active in several local trade and professional associations. She has even self-published some booklets for distribution to members of these associations: "10 Smart Ways to Purchase Office Supplies" and "How to Stretch Your Office Supply Budget." She often conducts seminars and workshops around these topics and regularly contributes to three association journals and magazines that her customers read. She also serves as chair of the local arts council and is an active member of her local chamber of commerce. She has been in the marketplace competing with Sarah for only three years.

Which one is positioned better as an expert, Sarah or June? Which is seen as a vital and valuable business asset? Which would customers be more comfortable in buying from, based on expertise and being positioned as a valuable resource?

Your personal positioning also includes such essential components as dress, style, image, etiquette, manners, timeliness, responsiveness, expertise, knowledge, and problem solving. All of these are things you need to pay very careful attention to on a regular basis. Is your car neat and clean? Are your samples or sales tools organized and spotless? Are your shoes shined? Are your clothes pressed and clean? Are your accessories tastefully assembled?

This concept of how you want to be positioned incorporates everything related to the views others have of you—macro (e.g., expert or advisor), micro (e.g., are you always on time or are you late?), and mini (e.g., are your nails clean?). Overlook these things and your prospect will overlook you.

Timing

We've already mentioned this essential issue. But it's so important to your sales success that it bears repeating. Like positioning, it is rarely valued by salespeople. What does it mean?

In competitive markets, it's not unusual for a person or organization to quickly and unexpectedly need your product or service. They may have a sudden cash windfall or even need to dispose of end-of-the-year cash. Their entire situation can change in an instant.

When that happens, you need to be the person they think of when it becomes important for them to purchase your product or service. That means you need to build and sustain strategies that make that awareness happen. You must be their vendor of choice. In order to do that, you need to achieve top-of-consciousness status with your prospects. You need to find ways to be in front of them when they're ready to buy.

But you can't be everywhere all the time. So you need to build "sales surrogates" that are in front of your prospects when you aren't. You need to master digital tools that work when you're not, that automatically get you in front of your prospects. You need to be where they are. But you also need to be in their mind—all the time. Remember: this is the 21st century and digital tools are here to stay.

> **Top of Consciousness**
>
> When your prospects and customers think of your product or service, how do you stack up? Do they think of you first, last, or never? By achieving top of consciousness, you are able to be the one they think of most often. And that's the status you want to earn.

The Importance of a Consistent Sales Approach

It's true that sales is one of the most highly paid professions in the world. It's also true that most poorly paid salespeople don't have a consistent process or procedure for selling. What would you think of a surgeon who told you after the operation, "I didn't

Getting out in Front

Ways for you to be in front of your prospects as often and as unobtrusively as possible are essential to your sales success. This is important because you often won't know when they suddenly and urgently need to buy. Here are some of those tools:

- Your own digital newsletter
- A monthly letter with a small gift and response card
- A quarterly update or special report
- Participatory surveys, the results from which you make available to participants ("X% of our customers believe the economy is getting better," "50 out of 60 customers feel these industry changes are imminent")
- Thanksgiving cards, Christmas cards, birthday cards (mailed or digital)
- Your own Web site
- E-mail updates

The key is that your process must be consistent and persistent—but you must never be a pest. For example, never *spam*! You need to make sure that whatever you deploy is helpful, meaningful, and positive. Remember: you're fighting for mind share! But always fight fair and square.

have a process or system for this surgery—I just improvised"? You would probably have big doubts. You probably wouldn't feel good about receiving the bill, either, and you'd feel worse about paying it. Then, if you needed any more operations, you would probably find another surgeon, really fast!

How often do you say or do something in a certain way in the morning and make a sale? You then do the same thing in the afternoon, but it doesn't work. Was there a big difference between the prospect who bought in the morning and the one who threw you out in the afternoon? Of course not. The problem is that you probably improvised in the morning, stumbled on something that worked in that situation, and then improvised again in the afternoon with the same grab-bag approach. But because it wasn't tested, proven, and carefully developed, it wasn't ready for prime time and it failed the second time. Now you're back to square one, looking for another, new approach.

Don't Use Scripts

Don't use a scripted, memorized sales presentation or a never-ending, static digital slide show. These are nothing but electronic flipcharts. Inflexible presentations lock you into an approach that doesn't let you adjust your interaction with the customer in any way. Instead, you need a living, organic process that will allow you to modify your presentation as you learn more about your prospect, a sequential system that consistently follows the same format or process but allows you the flexibility to be sure your presentation is absolutely, 100% on target to address your prospect's priorities, needs, problems, or most important solutions.

If you don't know exactly where you're going, you'll probably wind up somewhere other than where you want to be. That's also true if you know where you want to end up but don't have a roadmap that tells you how to get there. You need to have a carefully prescribed strategy for both prospecting and selling.

The Six Principles That Can Guide Your Sales Career

Do you find it hard to believe that there are just six simple principles that can drive your sales career to unparalleled success? Yes, there are only six insider secrets that you can use to reach the level of success that most people only dream about achieving.

Things Go Wrong

John was convinced his presentation was perfect. He had prepared it a week ahead of time. However, it was very close to being his standard presentation and he knew it cold. It was composed of 42 slides, all carefully loaded onto his laptop. He double-checked his equipment before the presentation to be sure it worked and was satisfied he was completely prepared.

But, two minutes before it was time to make the presentation, he discovered a few unforeseen problems. And they weren't technical! He learned that instead of 50 minutes for his presentation he had only 20. Instead of being interested in the product he had built his entire presentation around, his prospect really wanted a different solution. To make matters even worse, the budget had shrunk by 30%. Unfortunately, John had nowhere to go. He had only one presentation. What could he do?

Outdated Techniques: Don't Use!
- "If I could show you a way to save money you'd be interested, wouldn't you?"
- "The sale begins when the customer says no."
- "An objection is the sign of a closed mind and a consequence of something that has happened far earlier in the sale."
- "Learn the ABCs of sales—<u>A</u>lways <u>B</u>e <u>C</u>losing!"
- "Memorize 12 ways to close and 15 ways to overcome objections and you will sell well."
- "Sell yourself first. All else will follow."
- "The one who speaks first loses."

Part of the secret is to understand that these secrets are really principles, not techniques. This is a set of universally applicable principles that you can apply consistently and regularly and that will virtually guarantee your long-term sales success. These aren't maneuvers or tricks that will work only once in a while and are so manipulative as to make them only marginally ethical and situationally unacceptable.

21st-Century Principles: Use!
- "Prospects buy for their reasons, not yours."
- "Finalizing a sale is the result of effective positioning, prospecting, pre-call planning, building trust, asking the right questions, selling value, and sustaining credibility."
- "In the absence of the perception of value every negotiation will degenerate to price."
- "Begin with trust and all else will follow."

Principle #1: You Must Have an Integrated Prospecting and Selling Strategy

To be a successful salesperson, you need to think strategically. So, first remember that successful selling is a consequence of the number of qualified prospects you are able to be in front of and how effective you are when you are in front of them. You need to master two essential definitions:

- Prospecting is the strategy and systems you use to get in front of qualified prospects.
- Selling is what you do when you are in front of qualified prospects.

To make these two work hand in hand, it is essential to understand, assimilate, and apply them as shown in Figure 2-1.

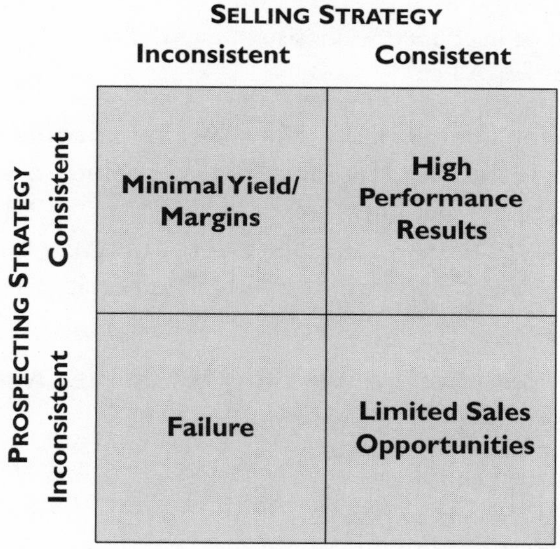

SELLING STRATEGY

	Inconsistent	**Consistent**
Consistent	Minimal Yield/ Margins	High Performance Results
Inconsistent	Failure	Limited Sales Opportunities

(Left axis label: PROSPECTING STRATEGY)

Figure 2-1. Effective prospecting and selling strategic matrix

The prospecting strategy, on the left axis, can be either inconsistent or consistent. Inconsistent means that you don't regularly, predictably, or continually apply the same, proven strategies that usually yield those prospects who share the five common characteristics of qualified prospects. When this occurs, you'll invariably have an inconsistent, irregular, and unpredictable flow of people to get in front of with your sales presentation.

Your selling strategy, along the top axis, works in much the same way. An inconsistently applied process or sales approach will yield the same results. You'll sell successfully only at times.

Tricks of the Trade

Equations for Failure and for Success

Inconsistent Prospecting Effort + Inconsistent Sales Effort = Failure

Consistent Prospecting Effort + Inconsistent Sales Effort = Minimal Yield/Margin

Inconsistent Prospecting Effort + Consistent Sales Effort = Too Few Sales Opportunities

Consistent Prospecting Effort + Consistent Sales Effort = High-Performance Results

At other times you'll falter badly. However, if you continually apply a proven, tested, and highly effective strategy on a regular basis, your results will improve.

Because both of these processes are so mutually dependent, you'll never be able to separate the two. The results? The diagram clearly shows you.

Principle #2: People Don't Always Buy What They Need; They Always Buy What They Want

Think about this for a minute. Do most people eat granola bars (what they need) or candy bars (what they want)? Do they eat bran muffins (what they need) or sugar-coated donuts (what they want)? Do they prefer to buy beer or books? Do they initially work to solve problems they really need to solve or the ones they want to solve?

Mistake Proofing

Knock It Off!

Don't start your sales presentation with the worn-out old phrase, "I'm here to meet your needs." Instead, simply say, "My job is to help you get what you want." You'll be amazed at the better, more attentive response you'll get. More about why this is important in the next chapter.

You need to be sure you're not falsely consumed by trying to address only your prospects' needs. Unfortunately, pure needs-based selling is a myth of the 20th century. If prospects bought only what they needed, there would be little room left for the emotional side of selling. Needs are rational, while wants are extremely emotional—and sales are really all about emotion, aren't they?

Some examples? You need a car. You prefer to buy the one you *want*. You need a suit. You buy the one you *want*. You need a vacation. You go to the destination where you *want* to go.

Principle #3: Don't Begin Your Sales Presentation with Unsolicited Small Talk

We have conducted in-depth research that shows beyond the shadow of any doubt that most prospects are put off by *unsolicited* small talk. The key here? If your prospect wants to engage in small talk, let him or her do so. However, don't be the one who offers it!

Have you ever seen how awkward it is to move from "small talk" to sales talk? It's like switching gears in a cheap car—awkward, noisy, grinding, and obvious.

Avoid looking for something in your prospect's immediate environment to talk about. Don't try to find "common ground." The truth is that every other salesperson who has ever been with that prospect has asked about the fish on the wall or the pictures of the children, admired the view from the office, remarked about the weather, or discussed the diploma on the wall. And every single one has been labeled as a "me too" salesperson. You need to avoid that label altogether. You need to be a category of one.

So, what should you say? It's simple. Just tell your prospect what you'd like to accomplish with your visit. After all, that's really the common ground that has brought you together in the first place, isn't it?

Here are three examples:

- "I'd like to have a chance to get to meet you and see if there is some way we may be able to help you."
- "I'd like to meet you today, ask you a few questions, and show you how we might be able to help you."
- "I'd like a chance to ask you a few questions, determine if

we can help you, and, if possible, show you some things that might help you get the solutions you want."

Principle #4: Most of the Selling Occurs Early in the Sale

The sale will be made or lost much earlier than you think it will. That may surprise you. It may also surprise you that most of the selling occurs at times when it looks like no selling is occurring at all. The first is the *pre-call planning* phase, where the depth of information that you acquire prepares you for an effective call. The other is the *questioning* phase, when you ask critical questions that allow your prospect to identify and verbalize what, how, when, and why he or she will buy. That's also crucial.

Smart Managing

Everything Starts with the Three P's

Never, ever overlook the important function that *prospecting*, *positioning*, and *pre-call planning* play whether you are calling on a new prospect or a current customer. That's because, in the competitive world of selling, the one who has the most information and who knows how to use it will usually win the sale. This data will also prepare you to ask the questions when face to face with your prospect that will allow you to make the sale.

In the face-to-face side of selling, the critical information that you're able to gather prior to the call becomes very useful

---

CAUTION!

Don't Stop Short

The tendency to stop asking questions before being able to prescribe the exact solutions that your prospect is seeking could prove to be fatal to making your sale. In fact, it's the biggest cause of failure for salespeople when they are face to face with prospects. Unskilled salespeople will ask one or two questions, assume they know their prospects' problems or needs, and then shoehorn a solution of their own design. The top pro, on the other hand, will draw out the prospect's most inner needs, wants, problems, and desires through meaningful questions and then prescribe a solution that is 100% on target to address every concern. That's the difference between winning and losing a sale.

as you begin the process of asking your prospects the most essential questions that allow them to tell you what they'll buy, when they'll buy, how they'll buy, and under what conditions they'll buy.

It may sound strange to talk about the three P's (prospecting, positioning, and pre-call planning) when you're dealing with current customers.

However, it's not strange—it's required! You must constantly be battling for mindshare, knowledge, and an advantage with both new as well as current customers. Don't ever forget: your best customers are someone else's top prospects!

Most old school salespeople will tell you that the

> **Mindshare** How much of your prospect's or customer's conscious or unconscious thought is directed toward you, your products or services, and your organization.
>
> Your goal? To own as much mind share as possible. Very much related to the top-of-consciousness principle, mindshare will dictate how much attention you will receive from a person.

key to the sale is how well you "dazzle 'em" with your presentation and how adept you are at learning and using multiple ways to close the sale. We have lots of research that shows the opposite is the case. We asked thousands of customers who had bought from salespeople what they would have had those salespeople do differently. The overwhelming response was "open the sale better." In another case, I worked with the top 100 salespeople from a sales force of 3,500 to learn how they closed the sale. Interestingly, the vast majority used one, single, simple, and easy-to-use closing technique—not 12. There will be a lot more about both of these issues later.

> **Planning Is Key**
> Never forget that the sale is generally won or lost *before* you get in front of a prospect. Also, never forget that the initial part of the face-to-face sale is far more important than rushing to finalize any transaction.

Principle #5: The Most Essential Face-to-Face Sales Skill Is to Ask Questions, Listen to the Answers, and Never Interrupt!

Let there be no doubt about it: sales is far more about asking and listening than telling and talking. But here's the problem. Most salespeople don't get it. They believe it's all about being talkative, persuasive, and verbally aggressive and having the gift of gab. But it's not.

> **Keep It Simple**
> Never interrupt a prospect. You, however, must always be interruptible. Ask the right questions. Ask for permission to write down the answers. Use more questions to determine the exact buying parameters of your prospect. Never forget: they will buy for their reasons, not yours. Then, you simply tell them what they told you. Selling is really that simple.

And to make matters worse, lots of salespeople (perhaps even you) have been told silly things like "You've got the gift of gab, you ought to go into sales" or "With that silver tongue, you ought to be a salesperson." Very few people are ever told, "You have the gift of asking the right questions, shutting up, listening to the answers, and then asking more questions! You should go into sales."

This is a case where conventional knowledge is all wrong. It's counterintuitive: what seems like it should work doesn't work and what doesn't appear to work will take you to great success.

Principle #6: You Must Have a Linked, Sequential Process That You Follow in Every Sale, Every Time, Without Fail

Far too many salespeople don't have the discipline to follow a sequential process. Also, far too many sales processes are too complex or confusing. Have you ever been taught the 12 steps to the sale, for example? The real fact is that simple is better. Shorter is also better. It's also true that less is more.

For more than 15 years, we have successfully taught a simple, easy-to-follow process that more than 500,000 salespeople around the world have mastered and used to propel their sales careers. It has been taught to people who sell both tangible products and intangible services, people who sell both big-ticket and less expensive products, and people who engage in both simple and complex sales. It makes no difference.

You, too, need a process that allows you to move through the sale easily and quickly, a process that will empower you to be in control, that allows you to know where you are going next in the sales process. Without a process, you will be inconsistent (remember that!) and so will your results.

The process that we teach is called the IMPACT Selling System™ (William T. Brooks, *High Impact Selling: Power Strategies for Successful Selling,* GamePlan Press, 1988). It is broken down as follows:

- Investigate—prospecting, positioning, pre-call planning, promoting, attracting
- Meet—engaging the prospect
- Probe—asking the questions so you can recommend a solution and make the sale
- Apply—recommending a solution that addresses your prospect's greatest need or want
- Convince—maximizing solid proof and allowing your prospect to experience the truth of your claims through third-party corroboration
- Tie it up—finalizing the transaction, cementing and reinforcing your sale, asking for the order

There are three simple rules for following the IMPACT System:

- Don't skip a step to get to any other step.
- Make sure you and your prospect are in the same step at the same time.
- Don't leave a step until you have completed that step.

There is no doubt that a simple, yet consistent process will work if you are diligent in applying it. This book will reveal in great detail exactly how to implement this process. It'll show you how you can sell successfully for fun, profit, career success, and prosperity.

As you progress through this book, all of the skills and strategies necessary for your success will be revealed in great detail. However, all of this valuable information will stay within the covers of this book if you're not proactive and diligent about learning, assimilating, and applying it. That's up to you. Let's move on!

Checklist for Chapter 2

❏ The secret to selling is to be *in front of qualified prospects when they're ready to buy, not when you need to make a sale.*

❏ Being "qualified" means the prospects have five critical characteristics:
1. They have a need for what you sell and are aware of it.
2. They have both the authority and the ability to pay you for it.
3. They have a relative sense of urgency about the decision.
4. They have a significant level of trust in you and your organization.
5. They are willing to listen to you.

❏ Smart salespeople don't waste a lot of time in front of prospects who don't have all of the characteristics of a qualified prospect.

❏ Being liked merely leads to selling price. Being trusted leads to selling value. Value is a far better selling tool than price.

❏ Prospects buy for their reasons and according to their time schedule for purchase.

❏ The two most essential components for closing a sale are *positioning* and *timing*.

❏ Six principles can guide your sales career:
1. You must have an integrated prospecting and selling strategy.

2. People don't always buy what they need; they always buy what they want.
3. Don't begin your sales presentation with *unsolicited* small talk.
4. Most of the selling occurs early in the sale.
5. The most essential face-to-face sales skill is to ask questions, listen to the answers, and never interrupt!
6. You must have a linked, sequential process that you follow in every sale, every time, without fail.

❏ The IMPACT Selling System™ consists of six steps:

Investigate
Meet
Probe
Apply
Convince
Tie it up

❏ There are three simple rules for following the IMPACT System:

• Don't skip a step to get to any other step.
• Make sure you and your prospect are in the same step at the same time.
• Don't leave a step until you have completed that step.

Focus, Alignment, and Leverage

"**I**'m here to meet your needs." It's as old as the hills and it's the way old school salespeople have been taught to open the sales interaction for years. But it's all wrong.

Over 25 years of research has told us an interesting reason why. As we revealed in the last chapter, people don't always buy what they need. However, they always buy what they want. Some more examples? Do more people buy whole grain bread or white, starchy bread? Do more people buy food from a health store or from the frozen dessert section of the grocery store?

Do your customers always buy what they need? Mine don't. Organizations need sales training. However, they don't want to go through the pain that's so often required to make it effective.

Let's take a look at your sales world. As a salesperson, you need to make sales. You need to make money. You need to generate income to support you or your family. However, you may not want to prospect and face the embarrassment of rejection or the sting of failure. Your customers may need your product. However, they'll buy—from you or from your competitors—

Needs vs. Wants

What's the difference between what people *need* and what they *want*?

Needs	Wants
high level of awareness	low level of awareness
related to a specific product	unrelated to any specific product
factually oriented	emotionally based

only the product that satisfies a want. They may want independence, freedom from detail, recognition from their peers, a sense of security in dealing with you, etc.

That's precisely why Chapter 2 suggested that you start your presentation with "My job is to help you get what you want." There is a big difference between what someone *needs* and what that person really *wants*. Smart salespeople know that difference and use it to their advantage.

It's All About Focus

Remember we said earlier that a salesperson can focus on only one thing at a time and that there are four possible areas of focus. It is possible to refine this even further. And this refinement has a lot to do with your sales success.

Focus A sharp, clearly defined center of interest or expenditure of time, energy, or money and one's capacity to sustain this targeted interest or expenditure over time.

You are really selling only two things, no matter what your product or service might be. You are selling *trust* and *value*. You're not selling your ability to be a likeable person who sells things at the lowest price—and that's a big difference between highly successful and only marginally successful salespeople.

Let's take a look at how this works across the whole universe of salespeople. Take enough salespeople, anywhere, and you'll get a normal distribution that looks something like this:

- 20% sell enough to barely get by or less
- 60% are average or slightly above or below average

- 20% are top performers, delivering 75%-80% of the sales

Where is your focus? What drives sales success? Skills? Attitude? Product knowledge? Luck? No, it's none of these. The major driver is where a person's primary focus is most of the time. And the bottom 20% of salespeople have a far different focus from the top 20%. They're concerned primarily about themselves and their survival.

> **CAUTION!**
>
> ### Where Do You Fit?
> You could be heading for the bottom 20% of sales performers if your primary focus is on yourself, your own survival, or a quota relative to phone calls, hours on the job, or any other short-term measurement. The bottom 20% have a focus on themselves that says, "I don't know if I can do this" or "Sales isn't right for me" or "If I just make enough calls …" or "If I can do enough to get by, I'll be fine."

The middle 60% have a focus that dictates that they pay most attention to their product, personal income, or ego.

The top 20%, however, have a very different focus. It's all about the prospect or customer. Within that group, there's a distinction: the top 15% focus on what their prospects *need*, while the top 5% focus on what their prospects really *want*. They're all about satisfying needs in the way that their prospects want to see them satisfied. The focus is very different.

Where's your focus? What do you pay most attention to? Figure 3-1 shows what defines your focus and where you fall relative to top sales performers.

Clarify Your Focus

To stay at the top, you need a philosophical understanding of customer focus and a sales process that allows you to implement this philosophy on a day-to-day basis. The IMPACT Selling System™ will allow you to do that. It's a principles-based, customer-focused, strategic process that will empower you with the selling skills necessary to keep your focus where it needs to be.

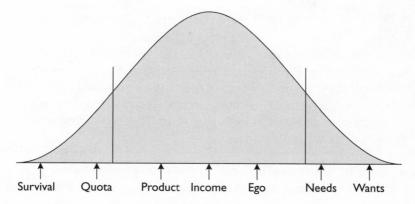

Figure 3-1. Focus and sales performance

Each step of the process has a very clear and carefully defined goal or purpose. You need to understand the purpose of each step and then achieve that purpose before

---

Changing Focus Endangers Your Customer Base!

It's extremely easy for your focus to change because of circumstances or situations in your sales career. Let's look at some examples.

How could the following circumstances force your focus to move from the customer's needs or wants all the way back to your own survival or a sales quota?

- Rumors of layoffs in the sales department
- A long sales slump and your job is threatened
- A sales manager who demands rigorous reporting on phone calls, call reports, etc.

How could the following circumstances drive your focus to product, income, or ego?

- A new product that you are told to push but you have no knowledge about how well it will perform
- A bonus placed on selling a certain product that customers don't need or want
- Needing to make two more sales by month end in order to win a cruise

Nobody said it would be easy! The irony? Focus on the customer and all of the situations described in this section will not be problems.

IMPACT Will Sustain a Customer-Centered Focus

Follow this process on every sale and with every prospect you ever contact and you will sustain a focus that is customer-centered. You will avoid the fatal trap of focusing on yourself (survival, quota, income, or ego) or your organization (product) and will stay focused on your prospect's needs and wants. That will separate you from 80% of all other salespeople.

you move to the next step. Perhaps the most interesting part of the process is to understand that each step is totally customer-focused. Let's take a look at each step again, in more detail.

- Investigate—to discover and attract those prospects who are most receptive to, need, and want your product or service.
- Meet—to build trust and develop rapport with the most qualified prospects.
- Probe—to ask questions of the prospects to determine what they'll buy, when they'll buy, and under what conditions they'll buy.
- Apply—to prescribe the exact application of your product or service in such a way that it will address their specific issues, needs, wants, and desires.
- Convince—to ensure that the prospects believe and accept what you say as being accurate and correct.
- Tie it up—to ask prospects to make purchase decisions when they are ready to do so.

Build Your Sales Philosophy

If you are going to have a great career in sales, you'll have to develop an overall direction or philosophy of selling. That philosophy will then guide you through the good times and the bad times.

There is no doubt that professional selling can be a great career. However, top sales professionals understand that sales is all about three specific things:

- Being consistent
- Selling at the highest margin
- Selling significant volumes of your product or service

If you constantly aim for consistency, you will be a step ahead of many other salespeople. That means consistent prospecting, consistently delivering high-quality impact-driven presentations, servicing accounts, and being dependable, delivering on time, every time.

Selling large volumes at high margin is what will also differentiate you from others and your competitors. Don't cave in at the first mention of price. Also, don't be so rigid that you would rather walk away from a sale than to work with your prospect on terms, conditions, or, at the last resort, price. There is a fine

Bob and Rachael

Bob considers himself a top professional salesperson. He's proud of never giving in on price. However, he's lost quite a few sales over the past year or so because he was so rigid that he wouldn't work with prospects to modify terms, conditions of the sale, delivery dates, extended warranty, or even price. The result? His sales are all profitable. However, he went from being #1 in sales to #8 (out of 10 salespeople in his company) over several months: #2 in January, #7 in February, #5 in March, #1 in April, #9 in May. What does that tell you about Bob?

Rachael is a very nice person—perhaps too nice. She sells piles of her company's product. And she is generally #1 or #2 in sales volume every month. Unfortunately, the profitability on her sales is poor. She underprices to make the sale, gives away product, provides extended warranty services at no charge, and personally overservices her accounts. The problem? Her company loses money on every sale.

Which of these two would you want on your sales team? Isn't it a shame that we can't take a little of Bob and a little of Rachael and make the ideal salesperson? Maybe we can. That ideal salesperson could be you, when you're armed with this knowledge!

balance between the two types of salespeople.

Leverage Your Time, Talent, Resources, and Advantage

In order for you to grow your territory or overall sales, there is a three-part strategy that could redefine your sales career and serve you well for the rest of your life.

There are, in fact, only three ways for you to sell consistently at high margin and at high volume. But to do this, you will need to prospect consistently, sell regularly and persistently, and service those accounts you win with great zest and vigor.

To implement this strategy, you'll need to disregard some old ways of thinking. Like the old belief that you should "underpromise and overdeliver." Instead, you'll need to learn to "promise a lot and deliver even more." You'll need to work a little harder, longer, and smarter than most people.

It would certainly be easier if I could promise you that you could have twice the income with half the work. However, sales isn't like that—at least at first. Unfortunately, even if you are successful, it never gets a lot easier.

Here's the three-part strategy that will allow you to guarantee that you won't be spending your day working on the wrong things. Instead, you'll be working at leveraging those strengths that you have.

The Three-Part Sales Success Strategy

- *Work* to consistently win more customers at high margin.
- *Work* to service those customers at a level that exceeds their expectations.
- *Work* to build sustained loyalty to vertically integrate those customers and earn strong referrals from them.

There are only four things you can do with your time. You can invest it, spend it, waste it, or abuse it. The problem? As a sales professional, time is your only real inventory. It is your greatest asset if you invest it wisely, and it can be your great-

How the Three-Part Strategy Could Fail

- What happens to this strategy if you don't get enough customers in the first place?
- What happens if you don't establish a threshold of accepting no less than full margin when someone becomes a customer?
- What happens if you overpromise and underdeliver?
- What happens if you can't build customer loyalty?
- What happens if you can't vertically integrate your customers (sell them more)?
- What happens if disappointed customers won't serve as referral sources?
- What happens if you're not willing to work hard enough to make all of this succeed?

If this three-part strategy fails, it's your fault! It's not the fault of the strategy!

est enemy if you waste or abuse it. Lots of salespeople just spend it, believing that there will always be more. However, that's false logic. Because you can't manufacture, buy, or trade for more time. You get all there is. So you need to leverage your time as best you can ... prospecting, selling, and servicing accounts.

What Do You Do with Your Time?

To succeed at sales, you need to be proactive and guard your time jealously. You need to invest your time, not just spend it. You need to avoid wasting or abusing your time. What are some ways that salespeople waste or abuse time?
- Failing to prospect
- Talking to too many people superficially
- Complaining about their manager, job, or product to other salespeople
- Spreading rumors and gossip
- Taking too much time getting ready
- Being disorganized

To be successful, concentrate on all the right things. Don't do the wrong things.

Your Personal Sales Talent Audit

To maximize your talent, you need to identify the talents you have. The most successful salespeople in the world are those who are most aware of their strengths. They also know their shortcomings, they work on them, and they avoid relying on them until they have made them into assets.

Here is a short, self-scoring audit. Please be as honest as you can about yourself. The only way to improve at anything is to have a baseline that says, "I'm good at this and not so good at that." People who refuse to face the truth rarely improve at anything. And professional selling is all about continuous improvement.

I consider the following to be a great strength that I have:
(Yes No Not Applicable)

Yes	No	N/A	
❏	❏	❏	1. Prospecting for new business
❏	❏	❏	2. Positioning myself as an expert
❏	❏	❏	3. Pre-call planning for calls
❏	❏	❏	4. Product knowledge
❏	❏	❏	5. Effective travel planning
❏	❏	❏	6. Developing internal support with accounts
❏	❏	❏	7. Building and sustaining trust
❏	❏	❏	8. Listening
❏	❏	❏	9. Asking strong questions
❏	❏	❏	10. Not interrupting prospects
❏	❏	❏	11. Making targeted presentations
❏	❏	❏	12. Creating and selling value
❏	❏	❏	13. Presenting my product with confidence
❏	❏	❏	14. Being persuasive without being boring
❏	❏	❏	15. Finalizing transactions
❏	❏	❏	16. Satisfying customers
❏	❏	❏	17. Delivering more than expected
❏	❏	❏	18. Selling current customers more
❏	❏	❏	19. Gaining referrals from customers
❏	❏	❏	20. Sustaining a meaningful relationship with customers
❏	❏	❏	21. Feeling good about being a salesperson

What Your Score Means
Let's take a look at your score and what it means. If you had between 18-21 Yes answers, congratulations! You're well on your way to sales success. If you scored less than 14, you might need some help.

What do the various questions ask? The first 20 dealt with the IMPACT Selling System: questions 1-6 with the Investigate step, questions 7-8 with the Meet step, questions 9-10 with the Probe step, questions 11-14 with the Apply and Convince steps, and questions 15-20 with the Tie-it-up step. The final question was a straightforward question on how you feel about sales as a profession.

How did you do? What are your strengths? Weaknesses? What will you do about them?

Leveraging your resources and advantages is all about how you maximize the tools you have at your disposal. Your resources include such things as sales aids and tools, digital equipment, and your knowledge, while your advantages include your product superiority, branding, market penetration, positioning, and all of those things that make selling your product or service for your organization easier, better, or more attractive than for your competitors.

Sales is all about leverage. Learn to leverage what you have and you will experience greater and greater sales success. Sales is not about obsessing over the things you don't have. Great salespeople don't invest a lot of their valuable time dealing with things over which they have no control. Instead, they learn how

Identifying Your Advantages

Effective salespeople are extremely knowledgeable about the resources available to them and maximize the application of these resources in their day-to-day sales activity. What resources do you have available and how effectively are you using them? Do you need more? What are they? How will you get them?

What advantages do you have in the marketplace? Your products? Delivery? Service? Warranty? Strong brand? Pricing? Technical Support? One-stop shopping? Your expertise? Are you leveraging your advantages? If not, why not? How could you do it better?

to create a career that is based on those things they can control—and then take action with their tools and advantages.

Checklist for Chapter 3

❏ Customers don't buy what they *need;* they buy what they
want.

❏ You are really selling only two things: *trust* and *value.*

❏ The bottom 20% of sales performers focus on themselves.
The middle 60% focus on their product, personal income, or
their ego. The top 20% of sales performers focus on their
prospects or customers.

❏ The IMPACT Selling System™ is a principles-based customer-
focused, strategic process that will empower you with the selling skills necessary to keep your focus where it needs to be:
  • Investigate—to discover and attract those prospects who
  are most receptive to, need, and want your product or
  service.
  • Meet—to build trust and develop rapport with the most
  qualified prospects.
  • Probe—to ask questions of the prospects to determine
  what they'll buy, when they'll buy, and under what conditions they'll buy.
  • Apply—to prescribe the exact application of your product
  or service in such a way that it will address their specific
  issues, needs, wants, and desires.
  • Convince—to ensure that the prospects believe and
  accept what you say as being accurate and correct.
  • Tie it up—to ask prospects to make purchase decisions
  when they are ready to do so.

❏ The three specific things that will help you build your sales
philosophy: being consistent, selling at the highest margin,
and selling significant volume of your product or service.

❏ The three-part sales success strategy: work to consistently
win more customers at high margin, work to service those

customers at a level that exceeds their expectations, and work to build sustained loyalty to vertically integrate your customers and earn strong referrals from them.

❑ Do a personal sales talent audit to determine your strengths and weaknesses as a salesperson.

The Investigate Step (Part 1)— Positioning

Investigate: To gather sufficient information about your market and individual prospects within it to enable you to make the best possible sales presentation.

The first part of the Investigate step of the IMPACT Selling System is about properly positioning yourself, your product, and your organization.

The real issue is not how often you tell your story. The secret is when you tell it, how you are positioned when you tell it, and how often you are able to tell it to the right people. It's the difference between looking everywhere for opportunities and creating your own opportunities with the right people.

There's an old adage in sales that goes like this: "Its not important who you know. It's important who knows you!" What does that mean? Simply this: you need to create a presence, awareness, and recognition in the minds of your buyers that makes them think of you first, foremost, and most receptively when it comes time for them to make a purchase decision about your product or service. This is called *personal positioning*.

The Power of Personal Positioning

In order for you to be the salesperson of choice, there are a number of things you must do. This is extremely critical because of the huge number of choices, options, and alternatives that buyers have in today's highly competitive marketplace.

This power of personal positioning is a weapon with great potential if you choose to use it. It can crush your competition. Take a page from the powerful marketing strategies of well-positioned companies and put the power of positioning on your side.

> **Key Term**
>
> **Personal positioning**
> How your prospects and customers perceive you relative to all other salespeople who can sell a similar product or service to them. It's presence, awareness, and recognition.
> What is your goal with personal positioning? It is to be the first, foremost, and most predominant choice in the minds of your prospects and customers. It's just that simple.

Personal positioning is all about three things:

1. Perception
2. Choice
3. Primacy

It's all about creating a perception in the marketplace that you are everywhere. And the more targeted your niche, the easier it is to create that perception. It's all about making your targeted segments believe that you and your organization are the suppliers of choice and that they would be foolish not to do business with you. And it's all about you being the person they hear from or about first, last, and always—the expert.

With the magic of digital tools and the accuracy to identify your specific market, all of this is possible, inexpensively and easily. Remember this: to your niched buyers, your personal positioning can supersede the positioning of your product, service, or organization—because to them you are your product, service, or organization. But you have to create the image you want them to have of you.

10 Ways to Better Positioning

Let's take a look at some ways that you can position yourself as being even bigger and all-encompassing than you really are. Here are 10 ways to accomplish just that:

1. Become a columnist for trade magazines your prospects and customers read.
2. Author a how-to-do-it manual that helps your customers do what they do better.
3. Develop and distribute your own monthly or quarterly electronic newsletter to targeted prospects.
4. Build and promote your own Web site with free information and tips for customers and prospects.
5. Send up-to-the-minute news releases related to your successes to media outlets your customers read, view, or listen to.
6. Develop your top 20-40 list of prospects and customers and send a monthly update, small gift, tip sheet, or relevant article.
7. Serve on appropriate boards and committees that have high visibility with your targeted prospects.
8. Offer to provide free how-to-do-it, noncommercial seminars or workshops for associations and organizations your prospects belong to.
9. Personally sponsor activities that are attended by people in your targeted market.
10. Create strategic partnerships with noncompeting products or services, to be seen as part of a total solution to solve your mutual prospects' problems.

All of these strategies have been used successfully by salespeople all over the world. There's only one question. Do you see any value in them? If you do, then the only remaining issue is whether or not you'll put in the time, effort, and work required to turn concepts into realities.

Don't Do It All

Don't try to do all of these things at once. You're far better identifying which one or two you want to undertake and have success with those than to have marginal success doing a lot of things poorly.

Decide which one or two of the 10 would work best with your market and determine if you have the expertise and commitment to do them. If you don't have the expertise, study, learn, or seek out others to help you. That's easy. Now, are you ready to make the commitment?

Six Ways to Misposition Yourself

How can you position yourself poorly in your market? Let's take a look at six ways that salespeople traditionally misposition themselves. If you do any of these things, you'll have trouble maximizing margin, selling volume, or building your business. Avoid these things:

- Too much cold calling
- Appearing as a pest to your prospects
- Coming across as desperate to make a sale
- Fitting the stereotype of the fast-talking salesperson
- Portraying yourself as a price cutter
- Being a product pusher

Let's take a look at how each one of these mistakes can derail your sales career.

Too much cold calling. Although some cold calling may be necessary early in your sales career, smart salespeople do all in their power to abandon this strategy as quickly as possible. Not only is this practice tough to do everyday, but the chances of uncovering qualified prospects through this method are very slim.

Another problem with cold calling is that it positions you as a person who

Cold calling Making phone calls, drop-in visits, or any other type of uninvited solicitation of prospects about whom you know very little and who have no idea about you, your organization, or your product or service.

is desperate for business and whose services aren't in great demand. The prospects think, "Don't you have anything better to do with your time?" It totally mispositions you.

Appearing as a pest to your prospects. There's a fine line between being persistent and being a pest. Think about that for a minute. What would you think of a person who was unpleasantly persistent? Who called you incessantly? Would you see that person as a professional whose expertise and time are valuable—or as an unpleasant pest who simply doesn't get the message to stop bothering you? The problem is that motivational speakers and authors have, for years, told you to be persistent. And they're right, aren't they? Of course not!

Coming across as desperate to make a sale. Let's take a look at an example. How much confidence would you have in a doctor who stood out in the street and waved down potential patients? There's an old line, "Never let 'em see you sweat." You may be in desperate need of business, but you must never give the impression that you are. That's tough to do. However, letting the whole world know you're so desperate is a fatal error.

Fitting the stereotype of the fast-talking salesperson. Let's face it. There are stereotypes for any profession or group of people, including salespeople. The stereotype of the backslapping, approval-seeking, fast-talking salesperson is not going to help to position you as a solid, powerful professional. In fact, the best way to position yourself is exactly the opposite of this stereotype.

Portraying yourself as a price cutter. The low-price provider has only one way to go in the market—out of it. What does that mean? Sales is all about margin, not just volume. Seriously professional salespeople position themselves as problem solvers and solution providers, not price cutters. Discounters, as a rule, have a short life in the marketplace. They stay competitive until they run out of money. Don't join them.

Being a product pusher. Your prospects aren't buying your products. Instead, they're buying what your products will do for them. In order to be able to provide that to them, you need to know what your prospects want to achieve with your products. Is it peace of mind? Profit? Pain elimination or reduction? Status? You also need to know how your product will provide answers to whatever problem your prospects are trying to solve.

> **Trade Secrets**
>
> Top-selling, smart sales professionals take great care to position themselves in ways that are consistent with the image and positioning of their product or service. That means that you need to be very careful about things like your dress, choice of accessories, personal hygiene, neatness, punctuality, and grammar. You even need to ensure that your business cards are clean, have no bent edges, and have no notes or writing of any sort on the back!

How to Position Yourself as an Expert

There's no secret here. To position yourself as an expert, you must be an expert. But what are those things you need to be expert about? A big part of it is to be an expert about your product or service. However, being an expert about what you sell means far more than having just product knowledge.

It also means that you need to be an expert in the following areas:

> **Product Knowledge**
>
> This isn't how much you know about your product or service. Instead, it is how good you are at accessing what you know from your mental data bank about what you sell and then putting what you have accessed in terms that are both meaningful and relevant to your prospect.

- What are the most common questions you get about your product or service? Your organization? Its history? Your service or delivery?
- How competitive is your marketplace? Who's your toughest competition? How are you different or better? How do your prices compare?
- What's the future of your industry? What are the trends? How does your organization fit into it?

Pro Positioning

In order to be positioned as a professional, you must do the things professionals do. That means that you should do the following:

- Research the organizations your customers belong to and join them. You may have to join as a supplier or associate member. That's OK.
- Read the journals, trade publications, and other newspapers and magazines that your customers read.
- Search the Web for information related to your industry and trends.
- Gather as much information as you can about your competitors and how they do business. Be sure to do this ethically and professionally. There's a lot of information available, for example, on the Internet.
- Ask other salespeople in your organization about what they see going on. Ask them about trends, the most common questions they're asked, unique ways to present your product, or how they are serving their customers better.
- Work longer and harder than your competitors. Read at night. Go to the Web early in the morning. It's all available 24/7!

- How does your prospect stand to benefit in light of future trends? What are the possibilities of potential disasters—economic or otherwise?

Here's the bottom line. You have to master your understanding of not only your product or service, but also the marketplace, trends, future possibilities, competitive factors, and much, much more.

Dress, Style, and Image

What about this thing called "dress, style, and image"?

How important to your personal positioning is how you look? To answer, let me ask you a few questions. How important is it for a restaurant to present an attractive plate of food? How important is it for a military band to march in straight columns, wear finely starched uniforms, play polished instruments, and follow a drum major who looks and acts as we all expect?

Yes, image is important. But what's the image you should project?

Should you dress like your prospects, so that they're comfortable with you? No.

Should you "dress for success" and look like someone who just stepped out of the pages of a fashion magazine? No.

Here's the answer. You should dress one notch above your prospect or customer. If they dress in a business casual style, you should be business casual, too. However, you should consider wearing a blazer. That would, of course, be appropriate for men or women. If they wear blazers, you wear a suit. If they wear suits, you wear a suit, too, but wear a shirt with French cuffs. The same, appropriate step up is consistent for women, too.

How to Dress Like a Pro

Top salespeople never underdress or overdress for any situation. Instead, they do their best not to come across as too casual or as trying to wow, intimidate, or dazzle by being flashy. You want to appear as a consultative expert who knows the importance of respect, style, and image. It's not about impressing prospects with your disposable income for clothes or accessories.

Always be sure to double-check everything before you leave your office. This includes samples, sales aids and tools, pens, business cards, and every facet of your dress.

Nothing looks worse than positioning yourself as an expert and then reaching into your briefcase to show your prospect a brochure you've promised and it isn't there. Nothing looks worse—unless it's reaching into your briefcase for your business card and there aren't any, so you take one from your wallet or purse, but discover that it's soiled or ripped or you've jotted down someone's phone number on the back.

How does all of this position you in the eyes of your prospect? You and I both know the answer to that question.

Stacie and Sam

Stacie and Sam sell local radio advertising. Both of their stations are top-40, contemporary stations in the top five in their market, with a pretty equal market share. Their rates are about the same and they offer similar advantages to their customers.

Sam loses about 80% of the time whenever he competes with Stacie—and he can't figure out why. Let's consider the facts.

Sam believes that everyone buys on rates, market share, and his relationship with them. He tends to push promotions. Also, he never takes time to wash his car and he spends as little money as possible for dry cleaning. He feels that understanding where radio advertising is going in the future has little to do with why someone would buy it.

Stacie sells outcomes that her prospects are trying to achieve. She works very hard at providing knowledge to her prospects and customers and carefully cultivates a personal image that's consistent with the image of her station—upscale and professional. When prospects see her, she is the station. She works hard to educate her customers about the value of radio, trends, and other means of advertising.

Does Stacie know something that Sam doesn't? And so do you. Maybe you know why he loses 80% of the time.

They're now placing a call to one of your competitors!

A couple of quick tips might help here. How will you know how your prospect will be dressed? It's simple. Call and ask. How do you dress if you are seeing several different types of customers in the same day? That's simple, too. There are salespeople who carry sets of clothes that they can change easily and can mix and match. They simply find a convenient place to change like Superman!

Positioning yourself correctly, however, can also be an "inside" job. Let's look at what that means.

The Role of Self-Image and Positioning Yourself

Your self-image is essential to your success. And the real truth is that you will never achieve any more success in your sales career or your life than your self-image will allow.

Remember when people said positive things to you earlier in

your life? Things like
"You'll be highly successful" or "You show great
promise"? How about the
opposite? Things like
"You'll never amount to
anything," or "You'll never
be as successful as your
sisters"?

> **Self-image** The conception
> that you have developed of
> yourself through your expe-
> riences, through things that people
> have said to you or about you, and
> everything that you have read, under-
> stood, or believed about yourself—
> good or bad, positive or negative.

How can you position yourself for success when you don't
see yourself as capable of succeeding? How about positioning
yourself as a professional salesperson when the common perception of salespeople is less than stellar? What if you share
that view?

Here's another question to consider. How do you establish
yourself as a professional in your own mind if you're expected
to sell in a slick, old school way, to use memorized phrases, to
handle objections with tricky maneuvers, or to close sales with
questionable tactics? You know the answer to that, too.

To position yourself for success, you first need to believe in
yourself. You then need to believe in sales as an honorable profession. Then you must also, legitimately, believe that your
product or service is the most viable, valuable, and logical
choice that your prospect could ever make. It takes a special
person to hang in there. And that person is you, isn't it?

Checklist for Chapter 4

❑ Investigate: To gather sufficient information about your
market and individual prospects within it to enable you to
make the best possible sales presentation. The first part of
the Investigate step of the IMPACT Selling System™ is
about properly positioning yourself, your product, and your
organization.

❑ Personal positioning is creating a presence, awareness, and
recognition in the minds of your buyers that makes them

think of you first, foremost, and most receptively when it comes time for them to make a purchase decision about your product or service. It's all about three things:
- Perception
- Choice
- Primacy

❏ Make use of some of the 10 ways to better positioning and avoid the six ways that salespeople traditionally misposition themselves.

❏ Top-selling, smart sales professionals take great care to position themselves in ways that are consistent with the image and positioning of their product or service.

❏ Product knowledge means understanding not only your product or service, but also the marketplace, trends, future possibilities, competitive factors, and much, much more.

❏ You should dress one notch above your prospect or customer. Top salespeople never underdress or overdress for any situation.

❏ Prior to going on a sales call, always be sure to double-check everything before you leave your office. This includes samples, sales aids and tools, pens, business cards, and every facet of your dress.

❏ Your self-image is essential to your success. You will never achieve any more success in your sales career or your life than your self-image will allow.

❏ To position yourself for success, you need to believe in yourself, believe in sales as an honorable profession, and believe that your product or service is the most viable, valuable, and logical choice that your prospect could ever make.

The Investigate Step (Part 2)— Prospecting

I nvestigate: To gather sufficient information about your market and individual prospects within it to enable you to make the best possible sales presentation.

The second part of the Investigate step of the IMPACT Selling System is about the actual physical activity of traditional prospecting.

The Differences Between Suspects and Qualified Prospects

There is no single effort that is more important to your sales success than the science and art of prospecting. It's a science because there are certain universal principles that guide and define success. It's also an art because it requires a carefully defined set of skills to succeed.

The truth is that your sales success will be in direct proportion to the number of qualified prospects you're in front of consistently and regularly. It's also true that when salespeople fail

Suspect A person
  1. With whom you've opened communication;
  2. Who may have a need you can satisfy, although he or she may not know it;
3. Who may or may not have the resources or authority to buy;
4. Who may or may not have any sense of urgency about buying what it is that you sell.
5. Who may or may not be willing to listen to you.

Segment A specific set of suspects who fall within the general niche you sell into. For example, if you sold office supplies, organizations that purchase office supplies would be your niche and your segments could be professional services offices, government, retail, etc. You could target certain segments. For example, if you sold medium-duty trucks, you might specialize in retail delivery, industrial repair, fleet delivery, etc., as your targeted segments. Good prospectors segment their market and then prospect each segment differently.

they generally fail for one single reason: they fail to have a sufficient supply of qualified prospects.

In order to be an effective prospector, you'll need to identify a targeted segment of your niche market that has a sufficient supply of suspects with the potential to become qualified prospects.

The secret to your success as a prospector is to be in front of qualified prospects when they're ready to buy what you sell. The fundamental truth is that people or organizations generally move from the suspect stage to the qualified prospect stage on their own time schedule, not on yours. You need to

Qualified Prospects

Smart Managing   In Chapter 2, we said that a qualified prospect is characterized by five common traits:
1. They have a need for what you sell and are aware of it.
2. They have both the authority and the ability to pay you for it.
3. They have a relative sense of urgency about the decision.
4. They have a significant level of trust in you and your organization.
5. They are willing to listen to you.

either be there or be the one they think of first or most often when that happens.

And the better positioned you are, the more successful you're likely to be. Part of this secret is to be the most visible option for your prospects. By operating within a targeted segment, the more likely you are to be the most logical choice. Bottom line: specialists generally do better than generalists.

The Three Most Essential Prospecting Principles

Let's take a look at three principles that, if you apply them consistently, can help you succeeed at prospecting. Here they are:

#1 The better job you do of finding and attracting qualified prospects, the higher your closing average will be.

#2 Your future success in selling is in direct proportion to the quality and breadth of your prospect file. The truth here should be obvious. However, there are some things here that aren't so obvious. For example, what does "quality" really mean? Simply this: prospects who have all five characteristics of a qualified prospect, who think of you first, fast, and foremost, are the highest-quality prospects. What about breadth? That means that you must be active and highly visible in a segment that's

John and Bill

John was the top salesperson in his 10-person office year in and year out, good economy, bad economy, good times, or bad times—it made no difference. Bill, a young, aspiring salesperson, was curious about how he did it. One day Bill asked John the inevitable question—how many prospects he had to be in front of in order to make one sale. In other words, what was John's "closing ratio"? Bill expected John to say that he needed to be in front of three or four. But that wasn't the answer.

Here is what John said: "My closing ratio is in direct proportion to the number of qualified prospects I'm in front of. And then it depends on how good I am when I'm in front of the right ones."

Words of wisdom from a great sales master. And his sales and paycheck proved that this wisdom worked.

that's deep enough to support your sales effort or active in enough segments so that you will have the number of qualified prospects you'll need to support your sales efforts.

If you have enough quality prospects, your sales career is in good hands. If you fail to accomplish that, your career is in jeopardy. It's just that simple.

#3 The salesperson who asks enough of the right questions of the right people in the right places will always have plenty of qualified prospects. What are those questions you'll need to ask? They're fairly easy to remember and are the very same types of questions that investigative reporters are trained to ask. And they fall into the age-old categories of "Why?," "What?," "When?," and "How?" questions.

"Why?" questions are great for helping you prioritize your time expenditure as you determine the process that prospects use to move from suspect to qualified prospect status. These questions can also help you determine which approach you should use with a particular prospect or type of prospect.

"What?" questions empower you to have greater impact by helping you focus on your most powerful choices for prospecting power. They're extremely valuable when you use them with the most likely prospects you have. They're great to help you focus on the specific ways to get and conduct a powerful presentation.

Timing is, perhaps, the most underutilized tool that salespeople have in their toolbox. Perhaps you're guilty of the same error. You need to be sure not to set up appointments, for example, that might be convenient for you but inconvenient for

>
> **Helpful "Why?" Questions**
> - Why would this prospect be in a position to make a purchase decision now?
> - Why might this prospect resist buying at this point?
> - Why would my timing be especially good or bad at this point?
> - Why might I get a particularly good (or bad) hearing now?
> - Why would my product or service be particularly appealing?
> - Why might it be unappealing?

Useful "What?" Questions

- What will this prospect find most attractive about my product or service?
- What might this prospect find least attractive?
- What should I do to get this prospect's attention?
- What do I need to know about this person? His or her organization? His or her preference for buying?
- What will my objective be for the first call?
- What do I have to do to get an appointment?

Productive "When?" Questions

- When is the best time for me to prospect? When am I at my best?
- When is the most likely time that I will be able to make a contact with this prospect? When is the least productive? When is this prospect's schedule likely to be the lightest? Most hectic?
- When should I contact this prospect again if my first efforts fail?

your prospect. You also need to be sure that you don't get so short on prospects that you'll jump at any appointment whenever you can get one, no matter how weak it might be.

The best strategy is to blend your circumstances with those of the prospect and you'll both win.

"How?" questions are the most critical for you in your prospecting success. You'll find that a lot of your "How?" answers will spring from other questions.

"How?" Questions That Work

- How can I prospect more productively without hurting my face-to-face sales time?
- How can I be more effective at prospecting?
- How can I improve my prospecting skills?
- How can I maximize my skills in approaching tough prospects?
- How can I follow up on every prospect more effectively?

What Are Your Chances?

Our observations and experience over the years have shown us that salespeople have a far better chance of selling current customers more of their products or service, about a 1:2 chance. They generally have about a 1:4 chance of selling to a referral or a customer they've done business with some time in the past—and a whoppingly poor 1:14-16 chance of selling something to someone they've never dealt with in the past.

What does that tell you? Perhaps that you need a lot of qualified prospects if you're starting out fresh, with no current customers or a weak referral base. It also tells you that it's far easier to sell to current customers or referrals than to prospects who barely know you. Finally, it tells you that it's far more expensive, time-consuming, and gut-wrenching to fight your way through those 1:14-16 prospects than it is to work with the easier 1:2 and 1:4 customers and referrals. But you still have to do it, no matter how tough, demanding, difficult, or time-consuming it might be and no matter how long you are in sales.

"Who?" questions are the most valuable prospecting questions you can ask. The reason is that they help you identify those prospects with whom you want to work. In order to do this, there is a series of questions that you need to ask yourself. However, before you do that, you first need to identify the exact, specific segments you want to attack.

Three Conditions for Getting Referrals

Smart Managing There are three conditions that are essential if you're going to obtain referrals from your customers. First, they must be more than satisfied. They must be thrilled. They must be delighted with you, your product or service, delivery, warranty, and customer service. Second, you must approach them and ask them properly for a referral. Third, you must be prepared to help stimulate their thinking with the appropriate questions.

For example, based on what you sell, you may want to target traditional types of customers who regularly buy your type of products or services, to revisit customers you had in a previous job, to research old files for customers whose salesperson is no longer with your employer, or even to plow totally new ground for a completely different type of prospect or customer.

It may seem like we have been dealing with a lot of questions. However, you need to remember that prospecting and sell-

What Smart Salespeople Always Know

Smart salespeople always know:

- What qualified prospects they're currently working with.
- How many qualified prospects they have at any point in time.
- What stage of the sale each prospect is in.
- What the profit/margin potential is for each prospect.
- When it looks likely that the sale will be consummated.
- How much profit/margin growth can be forecasted from each prospect.

ing are both about the questions you ask and not the talking you do! And the most important questions are the ones you need to first ask yourself. These questions will aim you in the right direction and provide the answers you need in order to proceed with the confidence and clarity you'll need to be a great prospector.

Here are a few more questions for you to ask yourself:

When is the best day of the week to contact prospects of certain types?

For example, you might find that certain people are never available on Fridays, others might be catching up on business activity from the weekend on Mondays, and so forth.

When can you get the most attentive hearing?

Finding Your Target with "Who?" Questions

Identify the segments you want to serve and then ask these questions:

- Who are the potential people or organizations I haven't yet contacted who have a legitimate need for any product or service right now?
- Who are ideal prospects I can contact right now?
- Who is an ideal prospect? How do I define him or her?
- Who are existing customers with whom I can do additional business?
- Who are former customers or prospects I can contact?
- Who do I know who might lend time to those who fit my ideal prospect's description?
- Who do I know who has the most influence on the prospect I'm able to identify?

Are your prospects busier in the morning or the afternoon, for example?

When are you at your personal selling best?

Are you a "morning" or "afternoon" person?

In order for you to prospect effectively, you need to find ideal prospects. There are lots of sources. You simply need to choose which ones you want to use. Strong prospectors understand that they need to be in front of qualified prospects consistently and regularly.

There are many things you can do to raise your visibility with your prospects. You can send them standard or electronic birthday cards, seasonal greetings, or notes. You might consider inexpensive, memorable gifts. You can also send them pertinent newspaper clippings, article reprints, or newsletters. Your goal is for them to hear from you four to six times per year at minimum.

Six Ways to Stay Organized

In order to be able to stay organized, you'll need to do six specific things:

It's More Than What You Know

Margaret, a top sales pro, grows her prospect list through several unique strategies. She belongs to a group of non-competing suppliers, all of whom sell to the same customers. She and the others in the group meet for lunch once a month to discuss what's going on with the accounts they share. Just last month, she learned that one of her customers was planning a major plant expansion.

She hadn't been able to see them for over a month, but Jeff, who sold them a totally different product, had also learned from their mutual customer that with the new expansion the customer would be seeking other suppliers to replace Margaret's products.

Margaret has a lot of work to do, but at least she knows what's going on. What would have happened if she didn't have this networking group? Do you have one like hers?

- Develop a standardized system for storing prospect data.
- Create your own customer checklist of data you'll need on each prospect, unique to your situation.
- Store your master prospect list, either electronically or, at least, in alphabetical order.
- Create a tickler file or set up a digital reminder system to stay in touch with prospects at the right times.
- Use frequent contact (e-mails, newsletters, letters, calls, gifts, cards, etc.) to keep you and your products at the top-of-consciousness for your prospects.
- Never send anything in any way that doesn't give your prospects a chance to raise their hand and say, "I'm now interested. Contact me!"

Approaching Your Prospect

Approaching prospects is one of the most difficult steps in prospecting. How will you open the conversation? What will you say first? How will the prospect respond?

There are two keys to prospecting correctly. The first, as we've discussed, is how you're positioned. The second is having every tool you'll need with you when you get there. That's something we'll discuss in more depth in the next chapter.

You'll need to capture the interest of your prospect as rapidly as possible. In order to do that, there are a number of things you can do. For example, you can arrange an introduction from a mutual contact. You can make arrangements to meet under common circumstances. You can contact them via phone. More about all of this later.

Where Do You Find Prospects?

Before you do anything, you'll need to identify, locate, and contact prospects. Which sources you'll identify depend 100% upon what you sell and to whom you sell it. Let's take a look at some ways you can compile prospect data.

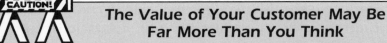

The Value of Your Customer May Be Far More Than You Think

Don't be afraid to ask current customers for help. If you have provided great value, they'll want to buy more and will be happy to refer you to others. However, if you haven't been working hard to service your accounts or have underdelivered on anything, customers will likely be hesitant to help you. As a sales professional, you need to realize the long-term value of your customers. What are they worth over the course of years in terms of sales, referrals, and goodwill? Never take a customer for granted.

Don't ignore the single best source of prospects you have—your current customers. Whether it's to sell them more, to learn about other sales opportunities in other departments or divisions of their organizations, or to ask for referrals outside of their organization, current clients/customers are great sources for more prospects.

Trade or local publications are frequently a good source of prospects. Based on what you sell, the business sector, community news section, classified, or even the personals can provide you with the information you need.

You may also want to subscribe to specialized publications for the industry to which you sell. Better yet, become a columnist and then send prospects copies of your articles!

It May Not Be Easy

When a salesperson leaves your organization, his or her customers can often be an excellent source for you. Every business loses salespeople and customers, but the losses aren't always permanent. Remember the ratios? Databases and files could be a potential gold mine of prospects.

There may be difficulties. You may need to prepare for some very negative reactions from some of these customers. Perhaps they're upset because they felt abandoned. In some cases, you'll have a tough time finding the customers. People move, die, change jobs, go out of business, and generally tend to be mobile and sometimes hard to find. It may not be easy, but the results should be worth the efforts.

Turning Lemons into Lemonade

Devise mechanisms for resolving complaints you uncover when you contact previous customers. Here are some examples of questions to ask:

- How familiar are you with our new, upgraded products?
- How long has it been since you last saw our new offerings?
- How familiar are you with our new customer service department?
- We haven't talked with you since (previous salesperson) left. How familiar are you with all the changes we've made since then?

Certainly, don't expect a negative response! However, be prepared if you do get one.

The Telephone

Sooner or later you're going to need to contact prospects. And the telephone still remains the single best tool for that. Some argument could be made for fax or e-mail. However, you want to avoid being known for junk faxes or spam that your prospects will throw away and for which they may resent you—particularly if they're unsolicited.

You may want to consider some form of pre-approach letter or series of mailings. The best way to do this is to have

Information Is Everywhere if You Look for It

Publications can provide you with information about changes in your community, important business trends, personnel changes, and more. This information can lead you to prospects. An announcement that an organization plans to expand is good news for people selling construction products, office furniture, office supplies, and placement services. An announcement of a promotion identifies a prospect for new attire or office decoration services. An engagement announcement provides a prospect for photographers, caterers, formal wear shops, bridal gown shops, banquet hall owners, and travel agents.

Web sites can provide the same information. Go to the prospects' Web sites and look for announcements of promotions, new product releases, earnings, and a lot more. Call the person who's the contact. Congratulate people who are mentioned: I'll bet that you'll be one of the few to do that. What if they're potential prospects? Who will they remember?

How to Avoid Telephone Failure

In order to be successful on the telephone, you need to master the following six skills:

1. The discipline to stay on task
2. The concentration to stay focused
3. Adhering to a systematic approach
4. Good verbal communication skills
5. A pleasant, engaging voice
6. The ability and resiliency to handle refusal and rejection

some sort of direct response mechanism that allows your prospects to respond to you in order to request more information. That way, when you call them, it's legitimate because you're responding to their request.

There are few things more disturbing or distressing than having to face a full day of cold calling on the phone as you are working from a list of suspects or prospects. Ideally, you should be responding to qualified prospects who want to talk with you.

Things to Avoid When Telephone Prospecting

There are some things that you'll need to avoid if you want to succeed at telephone prospecting:

- Making one call, then stopping for a break.
- Counting a busy signal as a completed call.
- Failing to call back after leaving voice-mail messages.
- Fiddling with papers, paper clips, pencils, pens, or your computer between calls.

There are a few more points that are important for you to remember. Never fail to get the prospect's permission to talk. However, never give the prospect too much information. Always keep in mind the purpose of your call. Is it to sell an appointment or interview? To actually sell your product? To arrange to send them some additional materials?

Give your prospect a reason to listen to you quickly. For example, "We help companies like yours double their productivity in less than 90 days." Be sure you're talking to the right person. Aim as high as you can! Be sure to gather as much information as you need.

You'll often run into three distinct scenarios on the phone. Here's how to handle each correctly.

- **You call and get a receptionist/secretary or gatekeeper.** Say, "I've got a problem and I need your help." People in positions such as these are trained to be helpful. Now, simply go ahead and explain your problem. For example, "I need to talk with the person who handles your printing purchases." Generally, you will either learn who the person is or be connected directly. You may merely want to learn the prospect's name so you can send some material in order to prepare him or her for your next call.
- **You're calling a referral.** Say, "Margaret Benson, a mutual friend of ours, asked me to give you a call and I promised her I would." If a secretary or a gatekeeper has answered the phone, say, "Margaret Benson, a mutual friend of (the boss) asked me to give her a call and I promised I would."
- **You call and get voice mail.** Say, "Hello, Ms. Jones. My name is Jim Rivers with ABC Widgets. We provide _____ to organizations just like yours." (Make sure you focus on *benefits*.) Now say, "I certainly don't expect you to return my call. However, should you be so inclined, I will leave my phone number for you, and I'll leave it twice." Now, take your pen in your hand and write your number on a piece of paper; don't give your number any faster than you can write it down. "My phone number is 555-231-3428. Again, it's 555-231-3428." Now, say, "Should you be in a position to return my call, I'll be available." (Leave the specifics here. For example, "Monday and Tuesday afternoon.") Here's the clincher: "If I don't hear from you within the next week, I hope you'll be in a position to accept my call next week."

When do you quit? Here are the facts. If you call someone three times and there's no response or you have no luck getting to him or her, your prospect is saying something to you: "I'm not interested." But all that means is that the person isn't ready now, not that he or she won't be interested later. Your job is to stay in touch with these future prospects. And you can do that electronically, with a newsletter, mailings, news clippings, etc.—all the things we've been talking about throughout this entire book.

Let there be no doubt. Prospecting is critical to your sales success. However, the way you initially position yourself will ultimately define how receptive your prospects will be to dealing with you. However, it doesn't end there. You now have to properly plan for your sales presentations so you can maximize your face-to-face sales opportunity. That's next.

But, before we look at that, let's talk about your single goal in prospecting. It's basically to "sell an appointment."

Setting an Appointment

How do you set an appointment? Let's examine it in detail. When you're prospecting by telephone, it's important to keep the conversation on track and moving toward an appointment. Unfortunately, you'll find that not all prospects are really easy to keep on track. You'll encounter objections and they may refuse to set appointments.

Let's take a look at the most common reasons why prospects raise objections to granting you an appointment. First and foremost is a poorly designed approach. You can solve that by understanding one simple thing. Your goal is to sell an appointment. Period. Nothing more and nothing less. In the structure of the IMPACT System, positioning, prospecting, and pre-call planning all occur in the Investigate step, to prepare for the Meet step. However, there's a secret here that you need to understand. When selling an appointment, you are really meeting and probing on the telephone. Those two steps are occurring within the Investigate step as well, even though you're not face to face yet. Build trust and then ask the right questions. But never be tempted to sell any of your product's benefits on the phone. Otherwise, there's no reason for your prospect to see you.

You want to build trust by asking if they're available to speak. Then ask questions like these to sell the appointment:

- How familiar are you with our organization and our products and services?
- What kind of a time frame, if any, do you have for making a decision or seeing potential suppliers?
- What are you trying to accomplish with a product like ours?
- I understand that your biggest problem is _____. What steps have you taken to alleviate it?

Then, move toward setting the appointment: "It sounds as if we can help you. We've helped lots of other organizations with the same issues." Now, set up the appointment. Ask, "Would Tuesday be good or is another day this week better?"

The second reason why you might fail at gaining appointments by the telephone is if you ask too few questions and do too much talking! Don't fall prey to this temptation. Ask—don't tell!

The third reason for failure is expecting the prospect not to grant you an appointment. And then, when he or she doesn't agree to see you, you aren't disappointed, because the outcome has met your expectations! What does that mean? Change your expectations.

The single biggest mistake to avoid is failing to convince your prospect that the appointment itself

> **Don't Give It Away** CAUTION!
>
> Don't ever tell your prospect too much about your product or service when selling an appointment.
>
> The most you'll ever say about your product or service on the telephone is that you believe that it will help the prospect. To learn more, the prospect will have to meet with you.

will provide a benefit. You need to ask the right questions and then provide a strong reason for him or her to see you.

Here's my guarantee. Use these exact words to get an appointment and you'll get great results:

How to Ensure Your Appointments Will Never Cancel

Here are things to say to guarantee that your prospect will be excited about giving you an appointment:

- "We have some great solutions to those issues you described. Let's get together and I'll show you how we can help you."
- "I'm glad to hear that you have gotten to the point that you'd like to solve some of the things we've talked about. I'm looking forward to showing you how we have helped others like you."
- "It sounds as if we might be able to help. When can we get together?"

Let's get together and let me show you how we can be of service to you and help you resolve the issues you're concerned about. But let me guarantee you this. If it looks like our product won't be a perfect fit, I won't hesitate to recommend someone else. Does that sound fair? What is a good day to get together?

Your goal in prospecting is very simple. To get enough appointments to guarantee that you'll be in a position to make enough presentations to qualified prospects. It's as simple as that. However, remember that there are three parts: positioning, prospecting, and pre-call planning. Let's look at the third part in the next chapter.

Checklist for Chapter 5

❑ Investigate: To gather sufficient information about your market and individual prospects within it to enable you to make the best possible sales presentation. The second part of the Investigate step of the IMPACT Selling System is about the actual physical activity of traditional prospecting and pre-call planning for presentations.

❑ No single effort is more important to your sales success than the science and art of prospecting.

❑ Your sales success will be in direct proportion to the number of qualified prospects you're in front of consistently and reg-

ularly. The better job you do of finding and attracting qualified prospects, the higher your closing average will be.

❏ People or organizations generally move from the suspect
stage to the qualified prospect stage on their own time
schedule. You need to either be there or be the one they
think of first or most often when that happens. Timing is,
perhaps, the most underutilized tool that salespeople have in
their toolbox.

❏ The salesperson who asks enough of the right questions of
the right people in the right places will always have plenty of
qualified prospects. You need to remember that prospecting
and selling are both about the questions you ask and not the
talking you do!

❏ Don't be afraid to ask existing customers for help. If you
have provided great value they'll want to buy more and will
be happy to refer you to others.

❏ When selling an appointment, don't ever tell your prospect
too much about your product or service.

❏ The single biggest mistake is failing to convince your
prospect that the appointment itself will provide a benefit.

The Investigate Step (Part 3)— Pre-Call Planning

I nvestigate: To gather sufficient information about your market and individual prospects within it to enable you to make the best possible sales presentation.

The third part of the Investigate step of the IMPACT Selling System is about the actual physical activity of pre-call planning for presentations.

Let there be little doubt. If you're the salesperson who knows the most about your prospect and are able to turn that knowledge into solutions, you're far more likely to make the sale than your competitors. At this point you've carefully positioned yourself for your prospects to perceive you exactly as you want and you've prospected diligently to get in front of the right person or people. Now you have to guarantee that your appointment will shine. Let's talk about how to do that.

Do Your Research

Salespeople, as a rule, are people of action. However, at this stage you'll need to slow down in order to speed up. What does that mean? You'll have to take the time to develop an in-depth, meaningful understanding of what you're getting into. You'll need to know as much as you can about each prospect before you get to the appointment.

You'll want to review questions that you've asked yourself. Among other things, you'll need to be sure you know the answers to questions like the following:

- Who are you competing against?
- What are their unique advantages? Strengths? Weaknesses?
- What is the buying cycle of your prospect?
- What are the budget constraints?
- What outcomes or solutions does your prospect seek?
- What are his or her prior buying habits?
- How receptive is he or she to new ideas?

In Sales, Knowledge Really Is Power

Joy was a top salesperson at her company and had consistently been number one yearly for sales production. In fact, last year she finished on top for the third year in a row. She won all the awards.

She was well positioned with her customers. She didn't prospect proactively as much as she used to because she had so many repeat customers. In the back of her mind, she knew she had to do more prospecting, but she decided to worry about that later.

But this year, it's a different story. She has lost three of her five biggest accounts. She's found out that two of her competitors uncovered that she had some service and warranty issues with those three accounts. She's also found out that the competitors who got the business dislodged her because they had started working on those accounts at the end of the last budget cycle, showing them how to spread the expense and improve the billing and inventory process. She also learned that the users of her products had told their supervisors (and her competitors) about the delivery and product glitches with her products.

How did Joy get "outsold"? What did she fail to do ... and what did her competitors do that she didn't do? And now, what does she have to do that she didn't have to do in the past, but should have been doing diligently?

This concept of researching your prospect also extends to your current customers. How well are you servicing them? How does your product or service stand up against the standard your prospect has set for it and that you have promised? Do your customers feel that they're getting the most value for their investment? Are you "defending the high ground," ensuring that you're not vulnerable to attack and the eventual erosion or loss of your accounts to competitors?

Researching potential prospects and current customers alike is critical to making an effective, powerful presentation. It's as simple as this: the more you know in advance, the better you can make your presentation.

The information that you gather must be processed into knowledge that you can use to your advantage when you get face to face with your prospect. But how can you use this information?

How valuable would it be to you if you knew about any one of the following 12 events before you met with a prospect or a current customer?

Sources of Pre-Call Planning Information

Smart salespeople will use every tool at their disposal to learn as much as they can about a prospect before they make a presentation. Let's take a look at just 10 possible sources of information:

1. Internet search for the prospect and review the prospect's Web site.
2. Annual reports, if available.
3. Trade journals, magazines, or newspapers with articles about the prospect.
4. People the prospect sells to or buys from.
5. People who know the organization through interaction of any sort with it.
6. People who work at your prospect's place of business.
7. Current customers who know the organization.
8. Prospect's internal newsletters or public documents.
9. Prospect's technical manual or warranty documents.
10. Prospect's promotional materials.

1. An expansion of facilities
2. A reduction or increase in budget
3. A change in a budget cycle or purchasing process
4. Reorganization or downsizing
5. Sale of the organization
6. Acquisition of another company
7. Promotion of an internal advocate
8. Termination of an internal advocate
9. Termination of a person who hasn't supported you
10. A change in philosophy either for or against your product
11. A financial windfall for your prospect
12. The entry of a new competitor onto the scene

Needless to say, if you entered into any face-to-face sale without some of this valuable information, you'd certainly be at a distinct disadvantage. However, if you entered the sale with this knowledge, would you be better prepared?

> **A Lesson from History**
>
> Napoleon: "To be outmaneuvered? Yes. To be surprised? Never!" Like Napoleon, smart, effective salespeople never allow themselves to be surprised by anything. Proper pre-call planning minimizes surprises. You need to take the time to research every prospect as thoroughly as you can to ensure that you are never surprised.

Developing Internal Support

Salespeople who sell well understand one thing: internal support can make or break the sale. They also understand that every organization (even a family) they'll ever sell to, whether it's business-to-consumer or business-to-business, will be governed by two things:

1. Formal structure
2. Informal structure

The formal structure is the way an organization is supposed

How Things Really Work

Productive salespeople understand the formal structure of their prospect's organization. And they never violate that formal structure. However, they do understand that things really get done through the informal structure. You need to understand the difference.

to work. For example, parents make the family decisions, the president decides, the purchasing department makes the purchase decisions.

The informal is the way it really works. For example, children are the ones who want to go to the fast food restaurant and receive the toys, not the parents; presidents of organizations get advice and input from those around them (sometimes the secretary); and purchasing departments look to internal experts to advise them on what products to buy.

Your Prospect's Internal Support Team

No matter what you sell or to whom, there will be four key players that you need to identify within your prospect's organization. No matter what the size, complexity, or nature of your prospect, those same four players will always be there. (It may not be four different people; one person can play multiple roles.)

Your job is to identify the four roles, understand that each has a part to play in your sales success, and maximize your relationship with each.

1. **Buffer.** This is the person whose role is to keep salespeople either out of the organization or, at least, at a safe distance from the source of real power. Quite often, this is a receptionist, secretary, team leader, purchasing manager, or product specialist.
2. **User.** This is generally a person who will be the beneficiary of the use of your product or service. Users may or may not have much power in the purchasing decision. You need to determine the level of their power or authority. Don't presume that they do or don't have power.

3. **Check Writer.** It's important to note the use of this term and not "decision maker." In many of today's more enlightened organizations, there are fewer and fewer people who could be called pure "decision makers." Instead, there are more cases where people are relying on consensus, input and involvement when making decisions.
4. **Internal Advocate.** Early in the sale, this role is the most important to you. You need strong internal support from someone (ideally several people) who can provide intelligence, guidance, outright advocacy, and, if necessary, subtle pressure on your behalf.

Interestingly enough, those fulfilling all of these roles can come from anywhere in the organization. It's also not unusual for you to garner internal advocacy from a Buffer, a User, or ideally the Check Writer. Frankly, the higher placed the person is in both the formal and informal structures of the organization, the better.

It's really pretty simple. The more prepared you are, the better you'll perform. Sales is a real pressure business—and the

Battle of the Prepared vs. the Ill-Prepared
Beth sells baby pictures. Margaret sells health food. Both sell to families.

Beth understands she's not in the picture business, but rather in the "feel good about my family business." Beth understands that if she can get past the decision maker's buffer (the "I can't afford pictures and don't want any" father) and garner support from the informally powerful, internal advocate (the "You'll want to have these memories" grandmother), she'll generally be a lot better off.

Margaret believes she's selling a better quality of life with her products. And she's right. However, she doesn't understand the power of identifying the key players inside the account. She has often said, "Everybody needs health food. I just need to present it to enough people and someone will buy." Margaret naïvely believes that a great presentation, no matter to whom, will make the sale.

Who do you think has been more successful in sales? Who will do better in the future?

worst thing you can do is to put pressure on yourself by failing to prepare properly.

Reviewing Your Resources: A Checklist

In order to show up at every sales presentation fully prepared and ready to perform, you'll need to ensure that you have every tool at your disposal. Here's a checklist that you may want to consider adapting to your unique situation.

- ❑ Relevant documents (prospect's annual report, brochures, promotional materials, etc.)
- ❑ Your notes on the prospect
  - prospect's phone number and address
  - background information on person(s) you're seeing
  - directions to appointment from your office
- ❑ Buying records (if a current customer)
- ❑ Double-check for proper dress
- ❑ Extra, backup clothes (tie, hose, etc.)
- ❑ Appointment calendar or personal digital tool
- ❑ Calculator
- ❑ Testimonial letters
- ❑ List of satisfied customers
- ❑ Necessary contracts or letters of agreement
- ❑ Anything promised to prospect
- ❑ Notepad or legal pad
- ❑ Pen and backup writing utensils
- ❑ Breath spray, dental floss (if after lunch)
- ❑ Pens, pencils
- ❑ Brochures
- ❑ Sales aids
- ❑ Business cards
- ❑ Delivery schedules
- ❑ Warranty documents
- ❑ Laptop
- ❑ Power cords
- ❑ LCD projector
- ❑ Connector cables
- ❑ Reference letters/list of references

Confirming Your Appointment

Never assume that your prospect will remember your appointment. Instead, do all in your power to ensure that you have the best chance of a positive, receptive hearing. You may want to consider sending a handwritten note or friendly e-mail to remind your prospect about your appointment. You may want to further confirm it with a telephone call to guarantee that you won't be wasting time by going to visit someone who won't be there!

Some might argue that this will give your prospect a chance to cancel. However, wouldn't you rather give him or her a chance to reschedule the appointment than waste your time traveling to an appointment that doesn't happen? Years of experience will show that confirming sales calls *is* a productive practice.

You're Only Fooling Yourself

Jason loves to live on the edge. The more crazy things get, the better. He's so good at this that he believes he can walk and talk his way through anything. And he usually does. He loves the excitement!

However, he recently lost the biggest sale of his career—a sale equal to four months of his regular sales volume. Why? He didn't know the sales principle that says the bigger the stakes, the more preparation required. He had no internal advocate. His competitor did. He didn't know how his prospect really made decisions. His competitor did. He showed up late for his presentation, didn't have the materials he needed, and was unable to produce a list of references when asked. He lost the big sale.

How would you like to be selling against Jason? How do your competitors feel about selling against you?

Mentally Prepare

There's a fine line between enthusiasm and competence. There's a fine line between spontaneity and memorization. There's also a fine line between overpreparing and underpreparing. Like lots of things in life, success really lies in balance.

However, to be successful in sales, you need to understand

Abraham Lincoln

TRICKS OF THE TRADE This insight comes from Abraham Lincoln. One of his great quotes went something like this: "Each day you get up and make a choice that it will be a good day or a bad day. And either way you'll be right."

What did he mean? Simply this: your expectations play a great role in how things will play out for you. Mental preparation can lead us to success or self-sabotage. How do you mentally prepare? What are your expectations?

the power of the relationship between preparation and realistic expectations as well as the role that careful preparation plays in your ability to perform.

In order to mentally prepare for a successful presentation, you need to be sure you're 100% mentally present before your appointment. What does that mean? You're either early or late. If you're not at your prospect's location at least 15-20 minutes early, you're late!

Why is that? You need time to relax, become familiar with the surroundings, mentally prepare, and visualize your success. Yes, visualize your success! There's no secret that mental preparation is essential to sales success. In fact, most of sales success is something that will occur in your mind far before it'll show in your paycheck.

You'll need to arrive early, get totally focused on the task at hand, become familiar with the environment, conduct a mental and physical checklist of your preparation, and then

Don't Be Like Mike

For Example The best way to ensure you'll be prepared is to avoid being like Mike. He recently made a sales call and everything went wrong. He didn't have correct driving directions, the previous appointment went longer than expected, and he arrived at his prospect's office precisely at 3:00 p.m. (the exact time of his appointment) and had to rush to set up his presentation in the conference room.

He spent more time apologizing than selling. He felt disheveled and disorganized. In fact, he never got back on track and rambled on incessantly until his prospect had to ask him to leave.

How mentally prepared was Mike?

visualize yourself being successful. Imagine how you'll feel when your prospect says yes to your offer. Picture the precise way you'll thank your prospect, promise to deliver, leave the prospect's office, and call your office and your spouse or significant other to tell them about your success. Visualize how you'll savor the congratulations, ... the awards you'll receive, ... the accolades you'll enjoy.

Visualizing your success is a powerful tool. However, you'll notice that we talked about visualizing your final success, not the process of making the sale. There's a big difference.

Imagine how you'll feel, act, and enjoy the fruits of your effort after you make the sale. Look at the end result, not the process. Conducting your checklist of the actual mechanics of the sale can often give you the added competence you'll need. Visualizing your success will give you the added confidence you'll need to confirm that you can succeed. Both of these— competence and confidence—are necessary for your sales success.

Physically Prepare

You'll be able to do this only if you're exactly where you'll need to be at precisely the right time that you need to be there. You don't want to be out of breath, perspiring, and rushing to prepare.

You'll need to understand the power of time management and organization to pull this off. But it's much bigger than that. Successful selling requires stamina and mental and physical toughness. You need to be ready to perform at a moment's notice.

If you haven't kept in shape, sprinting to your next appointment will leave you breathless, stressed out, and ill-prepared to perform. If you haven't physically checked and double-checked your briefcase, samples, and materials, you'll likely have a creeping doubt about whether or not you have everything you'll need.

If you haven't developed physical stamina or actually checked everything you'll need, it's obviously too late now. However, it's not too late to go to the washroom and double-

Making the Most of Those Vital 15 Minutes

Bill was making a sales call on a national trade association. He arrived 20 minutes early. He was offered coffee and, acting like a gracious guest, accepted the courtesy, even though he doesn't like coffee. He went to the men's room to double-check his attire and he straightened his tie, applied some eye drops to remove the redness from his eyes, and quickly buffed the mud from his shoes.

Then, while waiting, he noticed that the executive director had received a recent award (the plaque was on the wall) and that the organization had decided to expand by 20% (it was announced in the newsletter that was on the table in the waiting area).

How prepared was Bill? Did he maximize every minute of the sales call? Is the 15-20 minutes prior to the actual appointment time valuable? Should you consider it part of the call?

check your attire. Is everything straight? Little things make a difference: makeup, polished shoes, straight collars. Double-check everything.

Take a physical inventory of your prospect's surroundings. Do you see competitors' materials anywhere? Are there recent awards on the wall? How efficient is the office? How receptive is the gatekeeper or buffer to having you there? Are there items in plain sight that tip you off about things you need to know?

Preparation: Positioning, Prospecting, and Pre-Call Planning

Preparation is essential in any venture. In sales, it's often the difference between success and failure. That's one of the reasons why the Investigate step is such a large step. You need to devote lots of your time to positioning, prospecting, and pre-call planning. Fail to do that and your sales career will be mediocre at best. Great salespeople know that these three activities, if done consistently and persistently, can make or break a sales career.

Checklist for Chapter 6

❏ Investigate: To gather sufficient information about your market and individual prospects within it to enable you to make the best possible sales presentation. The third part of the Investigate step of the IMPACT Selling System is about the actual physical activity of pre-call planning for presentations.

❏ If you're the salesperson who knows the most about your prospect and are able to turn that knowledge into solutions, you're far more likely to make the sale than your competitors.

❏ Researching potential prospects and current customers alike is critical to making an effective, powerful presentation. The more you know in advance, the better you can make your presentation.

❏ Smart salespeople will use every tool at their disposal to learn as much as they can about a prospect before they make a presentation. They never allow themselves to be surprised by anything. Proper pre-call planning minimizes surprises.

❏ Salespeople who sell well understand that internal support can make or break the sale.

❏ The formal structure is the way an organization is supposed to work. The informal structure is the way it really works.

❏ No matter what you sell or to whom, there will be four key players that you need to identify within your prospect's organization:
  1. Buffer
  2. User
  3. Check Writer
  4. Internal Advocate

❏ You need to understand the power of the relationship between preparation and realistic expectations as well as the role that careful preparation plays in your ability to perform.

❏ To mentally prepare for a successful presentation, you should be at your prospect's location at least 15-20 minutes early so you can be 100% mentally present.

❏ In sales, preparation is often the difference between success and failure. That's one of the reasons why the Investigate step is such a large step.

The Meet Step: Engaging Your Prospect Face to Face

M eet: To engage the prospect and turn a potential resister into an avid listener. To develop trust and rapport while displaying your sincere interest in the prospect.

Engaging Your Customers

In the IMPACT Selling System, this is called the Meet step. This is the first phase of the face-to-face interaction between you and your prospect, and the real, underlying purpose of this step is to set the sales process in motion.

Your purpose is very straightforward: to engage the prospect and develop trust and rapport while displaying sincere interest in him or her. It isn't to allow you to dominate the conversation, interrupt the prospect, or "sell yourself." Instead, it's to allow several key things to happen:

- To build trust
- To build rapport
- To measure your prospect's receptivity

- To allow your prospect to carry on unsolicited conversation, if he or she chooses to do so

You have only seconds to establish your credibility and convince your prospect that time spent with you will be valuable. In fact, there's lots of research that suggests that time frame may be the first 19-34 seconds!

> **Key Term**
> **Trust** Your prospect's level of belief that you and your organization and products or services are credible and you will deliver on every promise or commitment.
>
> **Rapport** Matching the pace, tone, behavior, and actions of the prospect so that he or she is comfortable that both of you see the world in the same way.

When thousands of customers who had bought from salespeople were asked what those salespeople should have done differently, the overwhelming response was that they needed to open the sale better. Most people had no problem with the way the salespeople had made their product presentation. They weren't even concerned about being asked to buy. They didn't like the way the salesperson first engaged them.

Let's take a look at how you can do this better. First, understand one thing. Your purpose is *not* to get your prospect to like you. Instead, your goal is to get him or her to *trust* you. And there is a big difference.

> **Tricks of the Trade**
> **Trust vs. Like**
> Weak salespeople seek to be liked. They sell price. Smart salespeople seek to be trusted. And they sell value. There's a big difference.

In order to do this, you need to enter the face-to-face sale with the confidence that the Investigate step has given you. For example, if you are well positioned, your trust factor is higher to begin with. If you have prospected for the appointment in a way that is highly professional, you will be positioned in a very meaningful way with your prospect. And if you have adequately conducted your pre-call planning activity, your focus is now 100% on your prospect, not yourself or your problems. Attention builds trust.

It's All About First Impressions

Unfortunately, some prospects see a sales call as an interruption from the important things they want to be doing. Unless, of course, they see you as vital to providing the answers they seek, the products they want, or the solutions they need. You must avoid coming across as an intruder, a beggar, or a time-waster.

Fail to position yourself strongly and some prospects will agree to see you only to be polite or only as a favor. Unless you can change either of these attitudes quickly, you'll never get anywhere with your prospects.

That means that you must first reduce tension quickly. And, make no mistake about it, there will always be tension in any sales situation. If you have trouble dealing with tension, you'll have trouble dealing with sales. It's just that simple.

Inspire High Expectations

Does your prospect believe you have something of value to say? Prospects will pay attention to someone who they believe has something important to say to them. You need to position yourself as that person. When you do, your first impression will be a good one.

It All Starts with You

Prospects can read you like a book. They can instantly sense your confidence, your attitude about selling, your belief in your product, and your personal comfort level with them. It shows in your eyes, gestures, movements, and tone of voice.

If you don't relax, they won't. If you can't reduce the tension between the two of you, you'll never get to the trust level that is required. Yes, it all starts with you.

Eight Ways to Ease Your Inner Tension

Let's take a look at eight ways that you can begin to calm the inner you. It's essential to reduce the tension that you feel, because that inner tension will be directed from you to your prospect. You must feed your mind thoughts like these:

- My purpose is to help this person identify his or her biggest problems and to provide the answers he or she needs.
- I generate value for this person.
- I am a capable and confident sales professional.
- My organization and products promise a lot and deliver even more. My job is to help this prospect experience that value.
- What I sell has far greater value than the price I'm asking for it.
- I care a great deal for this prospect and my goal is to demonstrate that caring by carefully prescribing solutions to his or her biggest problems.
- Selling is an honorable profession that I am proud to represent.
- If my product isn't a good solution for this prospect, I'm fully prepared to end this interview.

These eight affirmations are powerful, proven ways to feel better about yourself, why you're there, and why you're doing what you do. They will enhance your inner self and your level of confidence as you begin to feel less inner tension and a greater sense of comfort.

Affirmation A present-tense, first-person statement that you repeat to yourself regularly. The more you say it, the more it finds its way into your subconscious. And your subconscious is the source of all you believe about yourself.

It's important that these affirmations are statements that you can back up with facts. When you start seeing yourself in that light, you'll be surprised at how much more warmly your prospects will welcome you.

But a word of caution. Before you dismiss these ideas as silly or ineffective, give them a try. Whether you've been selling for 25 days or 25 years, they are as critical to your sales success as product knowledge or technical selling skills will ever be.

Maximizing Trust

Let's take a look at three specific things you can do to reduce the lack of trust that can exist when you first engage your prospect.

1. Eliminate any potential tension inducers before you make the sales call. We've talked a lot about this, but it's certainly worth mentioning again. Make sure you look neat, you're dressed properly, you're punctual, you know enough about the prospect, and you have everything with you that you need to be fully confident.

   > **Key Term**
   >
   > **Tension inducer** Anything that can cause tension to increase in a sales situation.

2. Look for tangible ways to help your prospect relax. A quiet, confident manner and a warm smile go a long way toward lowering resistance and tension. Use them.

3. Be a good guest. When you're in someone's home or place of business, you're on their turf and you're bound by etiquette and courtesy to abide by their rules. For example, graciously accept any hospitality your hosts offer. Ask where you can hang a raincoat or topcoat. Place your briefcase on the floor, not on someone's desk. Ask for permission to place a laptop on a desk before you do so.

Don't Dominate—Participate

One of the most important things to avoid is dominating the conversation when you first engage your prospect. In fact, your desire to appear to be friendly and talkative and to be Mr. or Ms. Sunshine can sometimes prove to be as much a detriment as a strength. Quite frankly, our research shows that salespeople who dominate the conversation and offer too much unsolicited small talk are not seen in a favorable light by their prospects. In fact, quite the contrary.

Talk Is Cheap— But Often Costly

Unsolicited small talk is conversation that the salesperson initiates and generally deals with topics that are irrelevant, uninteresting, or boring to the prospect. On the other hand, solicited small talk is offered by the prospect about issues that he or she considers relevant, interesting, and exciting. Avoid unsolicited small talk at all costs!

Statement of Intention

Your goal is to allow your prospects to talk about things that are important and relevant to them. If prospects want to talk, let them. If they don't want to talk, simply move directly into "sales talk" by telling them precisely what you'd like to accomplish and why, by using the simple *statement of intention*.

For example, you might say, "I'd like to have a chance to meet you and ask you a few questions to see if we may have something that could be of value to you." At that point you'd simply move on to the Probe step. We'll talk about how to do that shortly.

The Bonding Statement

This is a concept that very few people understand or use. Instead, they have usually been taught to say something like "I'm here to meet your needs." We've said earlier that people don't always buy what they need; they will far more often buy what they want. So, why not tell them that you're going to help them get what they want? Here's a sample *bonding*

The Soft Landing

If you really (and I mean *really*) want to ensure that you build and sustain trust, an excellent statement to make following the statement of intention is this: "I can promise you this: if, together, we see that I can't help you, I can certainly recommend someone who can."

Think about this for a moment. You have told the prospect that you (a) just want to meet him or her, (b) would simply like to ask a few questions, (c) will determine if you can help, and (d) if you both determine that there is no way you can help, you will recommend someone else who can help.

statement: "My goal is to help you get what you want. And we've discovered that, if we do that, things work out best for everyone. Does that make sense?"

Putting It All Together

Let's take a look at the first part of this initial interaction with your prospect. Remember: you've arrived early, you're fully prepared, you have everything you'll need, and you've spent time orienting yourself and mentally preparing for the meeting. Now, you meet your prospect face to face. Here we go:

Hello, Ms. Johnston. Thank you for seeing me. I'd like to have a chance to meet you and ask you a few questions to see if we might have something that could be of value to you.

I can promise you this: if, together, we see that I can't help you, I can certainly recommend someone who can.

My goal is to help you get what you want. And we've discovered that, if we do that, things work out best for everyone. Does all that make sense?

Some prospects will say absolutely nothing. If your prospect doesn't want to talk, move directly into the sales talk we've suggested.

However, most prospects will say something! They'll greet you, offer a tour of their office, offer a cup of coffee, initiate a conversation, or even start asking you about yourself. That is *solicited* small talk. But remember—the small talk must come from *them*, not *you.*

> **Sales Unscripted**
>
> Top sales professionals don't memorize a script. Instead, they modify statements so that they are comfortable and natural for them to say. For example, learn the basic components and parts of what I've suggested for you to say and then adapt it so that it's yours and matches your basic style of speech and level of comfort.

If they want to talk, here are some tips that can help you make it more productive:

- Ask questions to get your prospects talking about them-selves. Nothing gets prospects more involved in the sell-ing process more quickly or effectively than inviting them to talk about themselves.
- Draw them out. As they talk, use follow-up questions that get them telling you more. For example, "That's interest-ing, tell me more" or "Could you expand on that?" or "What else happened?" are all great follow-up questions.
- Really listen to what they say. Look the person right in the eye and visually respond to everything they say: nod, lean forward, put your hand on your chin as you lean for-ward. All these actions are great ways to show you're interested and listening.
- Show a genuine interest in what they tell you by feeding it back to them. For example, "I'm sure that learning about your friend's illness was difficult, wasn't it?"
- Always remember that the quickest way to get people involved with you is for you to get involved with them. What does that mean? If they're ready to move into the sale, do it. If they want to talk, talk. If they want to give you a tour, take it. If they want to take you to the coffee machine for coffee, go.
- Gain eye contact and lock into the emotions of your prospect. Try to connect with what the person is feeling— about your being there, about other things going on in his or her life at the moment, and about life in general.

One of the best ways to get people involved with what you want to happen is to feel and show a real understanding of what they are feeling. Put yourself in the prospect's shoes and try to pick up on what he or she is experiencing at the moment. For example, if the prospect has a headache, imag-ine what it would be like to listen to a salesperson talk while your head is throbbing!

When you do that, two amazing things happen. One, you begin to actually feel a genuine empathy with what the person is feeling. Two, the empathy you feel is somehow transmitted through eye contact to the other person.

Some More Tips

Get to the point of your visit quickly. Four questions are uppermost in the prospect's mind from the moment you knock at the door:

1. Who are you?
2. Whom do you represent?
3. What do you want?
4. What will I get out of this?

Avoid being abrupt. Amateurs often say things like "Well, I know you don't have all day to talk and neither do I, so let's get down to business." Or they may have been taught to ask a startling question that is totally out of touch with everything that's been said up to that point. For example, "If I could show you how to double your return in half the time, you'd listen, wouldn't you?" In today's sophisticated marketplace, that's a great way for you to be thrown out, not invited to stay!

The real pros take a more balanced approach. They ask non-threatening questions or make statements that gently open the door.

Make it natural. Let it flow naturally from the rapport you've set in motion. Look for a tangible way to identify with the prospect and start from there. Search for a common interest, a point of personal pride or delight for the prospect, or a way to express concern over a problem he or she might be experiencing. Then, use that as a launching pad for your shift into sales talk.

Things have a way of becoming intensely interesting to us when they become personal. Likewise, salespeople become very interesting to prospects when they become personal in a nonthreatening way. But don't be artificial with it. False flattery, inane chatter, and insincere comments create tension rather than reduce it. And I'm not suggesting you fake an interest. If you are not genuinely interested in people, you'll have a tough time making a living in sales. But if you are really interested, all you need is to use a little creativity to find a way to express it.

By identifying with your prospects, you enable them to identify with you. You help to establish the feeling that you see life pretty much as they do and that you mean them no harm.

Building a Bridge

The shift from friendly conversation to active sales talk is one you simply must make, but when you make it, you want response—not reaction.

Perhaps the most helpful image that comes to mind is building a bridge across a chasm. The best way to move prospects from friendly chitchat to businesslike sales talk is to give them a firm foundation to walk across.

Obviously, the most crucial factor in building a bridge is knowing where you are and where you're going. One reason so many salespeople fail at building that bridge is that they start from the wrong place and/or try to get to the wrong place. They may start from a tricky foot-in-the-door tactic and try to set up the prospect for the "kill." It just doesn't work. A better approach is to start from a position of strong trust and good rapport, then build toward conveying value.

Someone once said that the bridge was one of the world's greatest inventions. That's probably right. Bridges are essential to a sale, too. A bridge will allow you to get from one stage of the sale to the next—in this case, from the Meet to the Probe. And it's not that hard if you know a couple of things.

One is the three rules of IMPACT Selling. Again, here they are:

- Never skip a step to get to any other step. You started with the first step, Investigate, and now you're in the second, Meet, and preparing to go to the third, Probe.
- Make sure you and your prospect are in the same step at the same time. You need to invite your prospect to cross

the bridge with you and be sure that both of you are ready for the journey.

- Don't leave a step until you have completed that step. You must be sure your prospect is ready, willing, and able to leave the Meet step and cross the bridge to the Probe step.

> **Your Bridge Ticket**
> Your bridge ticket is a simple question followed by easy-to-answer follow-up questions. If you get the right answers to those questions, you're ready to cross the bridge to the Probe step. If you don't get a positive response, you need to stay where you are, on this side of the bridge, in the Meet step. Stay here and continue to build trust and rapport. Once you feel you've achieved that, try again to get that ticket to cross the bridge.

How to Cross the Bridge

To move from the Meet step to the Probe step, you'll simply need to ask your prospect this question: "To see if we can be of help to you, do you mind if I ask you a few questions?" If your prospect says, "No, I don't mind" (which happens 99% of the time if you've been successful in the Meet step), you will then ask, "Do you mind if I take a few notes so that I have something I can refer to?" Again, 99% of the time your prospect will have no problem with that, either.

Why do you ask these questions? First, you need a transition to get to the Probe ("Do you mind if I ask you a few questions?"). Second, some people aren't comfortable with someone taking notes on what they say ("Do you mind if I take a few notes ...?").

Again, the purpose of the Meet step is to set the face-to-face sales process in motion, to build trust and rapport. It's necessary for you to have a firm base to cross the bridge to the Probe step, where most of the sale really takes place. Let's go there now.

What Do I Do?

If your prospect says to you, "I don't want to answer your questions," what does that tell you? Simply this: you've failed to build trust, you didn't know it, and you proceeded to the Probe step too quickly.

If that happens, simply stay in the Meet step and say something like "I can understand that. You know, I was really intrigued by your earlier statement about your _____ (horse, home, etc.). Could you tell me more about that?" Now stay in the Meet and allow your prospect to continue talking about himself or herself. Don't be too hasty to cross the bridge!

Checklist for Chapter 7

❏ In the IMPACT Selling System, engaging your customers is called the Meet step. Your purpose is very straightforward:
  • To engage your prospect and turn a potential resister into an avid, engaged participant.
  • To develop trust and build rapport while displaying your sincere interest in your prospect as a human being.

❏ In the Meet step, you need:
  1. To build trust
  2. To build rapport
  3. To measure your prospect's receptivity
  4. To allow your prospect to carry on unsolicited conversation, if he or she chooses to do so

❏ You have only seconds to establish your credibility and convince your prospect that time spent with you will be valuable.

❏ Prospects will pay attention to someone whom they believe has something important to say to them. When you position yourself as that person, your first impression will be a good one.

❏ Some prospects see a sales call as an interruption—unless they see you as vital to providing the answers they seek, the products they want, or the solutions they need.

❑ Affirmations are powerful, proven ways to feel better about yourself, why you're there, and why you're doing what you do.

❑ Three specific things can reduce any lack of trust when you start to engage your prospect:
  1. Eliminate any potential tension inducers before you make the sales call.
  2. Look for tangible ways to help your prospect relax.
  3. Be a good guest.

❑ Don't dominate the conversation. Research shows that salespeople who dominate the conversation and offer too much unsolicited small talk are seen unfavorably by their prospects.

❑ Your goal is to allow your prospects to talk about things that are important and relevant to them.

❑ Top sales professionals don't memorize a script. Instead, they modify statements so that they are comfortable and natural for them to say.

❑ When you make the shift from friendly conversation to active sales talk, you want response—not reaction.

❑ To move from the Meet step to the Probe step, ask your prospect two questions: "To see if we can be of help to you, do you mind if I ask you a few questions?" and "Do you mind if I take a few notes so that I have something I can refer to?"

8

The Probe Step: Asking Questions That Make the Sale

Probe: To have the prospect identify, feel, and verbalize his or her needs, desires, and wishes; to determine *what* he or she will buy, *how* he or she will buy it, *why* he or she will buy it, and *under what conditions* he or she will buy it.

Selling is really not that hard. The secret—as I've mentioned several times so far—is to be in front of the right people at the right time with the right solution when they need to buy it. What can ruin this scenario of sales success is the fatal flaw—to be so focused on what you want to have happen that you lose sight of what the prospect wants to have happen. If you fall prey to the fatal flaw in selling, all of your positioning, prospecting, pre-call planning, and meeting efforts will have been in vain.

Avoid the Fatal Flaw

There are two things that can cause the fatal flaw to occur. One is that your listening skills are poor and the other is that you fail to ask the right questions to learn what the prospect really wants to have happen. In other words, you may not be paying attention or you may lack the skill, knowledge, patience, or know-how to ask the right questions.

However, you can ask the right questions and still get nowhere if you don't

> **Avoid the Fatal Flaw**
>
> Don't focus so much on what you want to have happen that you lose sight of what the prospect wants to have happen.

have the basic, fundamental skills of listening. Here's a simple example. I could ask you what you'd like for dinner, when you'd like to eat, and even what you'd like for dessert and you'd give me appropriate answers very easily. But if I didn't bother to listen to those answers, my questions wouldn't matter, because I'd probably serve you the wrong meal at the wrong time with the wrong dessert. Are you ever accused of serving your prospect the wrong meal?

It All Starts with Listening

There is a big difference between hearing and listening. Hearing is the physical response of your ears and the inner mechanism that picks up sound waves and translates them into signals you can understand. Listening is the active process of deciphering signals and translating them into meaning. It's the precise opposite of talking. The truth is that most people are better talkers than listeners: they're much

> **Listen Actively**
>
> To sell well, you must be a good active listener.
> That means being attentive to words, tones, and gestures and translating them into meanings. Without that skill, your sales calls will be a "monologue in duet" or "dual, even dueling, monologues." You will only pay attention to yourself and never sell well.

more adept at expressing their feelings and concerns than at listening to the feelings and concerns of others. How about you?

Tips for Being a Great Active Listener

Here are some tested and proven tips to help you become a good listener:

1. **Open your mind and ears.** Switch off all negative thoughts and feelings about the prospect and be receptive to the messages he or she is conveying.
2. **Listen from the first sentence.** Don't be thinking about what you're going to say next. Don't be planning the rest of your presentation. Put aside what your agenda may be and give your undivided attention to your prospect.
3. **Analyze what is being said and not being said.** Even the slowest listeners can think faster than the fastest talkers. Avoid trying to figure out what your prospect is going to say; you may miss what he or she actually says. Instead, use your faster thinking speed to analyze what your prospect is saying.
4. **Listen; don't talk.** Active listening is not only a great selling skill; it's also an important interpersonal skill. Always help your prospect convey his or her meanings accurately to you. For example, paraphrase what your prospect has said to be sure you understand when it's your turn to talk.
5. **Never interrupt, but always be interruptible!** Nothing cuts off the flow of meaningful dialogue quite as effectively as continuous interruptions. What's more, it's offensive and rude.
6. **Ask clarifying questions to stimulate your prospect to talk so you can better understand what he or she means.** Show that you're taking him or her seriously by drawing out elaborations and explanations.
7. **Remember what is said.** Log important points into your mental computer. Look for connections among apparently unrelated remarks.
8. **Block out interruptions and distractions.** Concentrate so fully on what's being said that you don't even notice visual and audible distractions.
9. **Be responsive.** Get your whole body into listening and showing that you are paying attention. Look the person squarely in the eye and use facial expressions and gestures to show you hear and understand what's being said.
10. **Stay cool!** Don't overreact to highly charged words and tones. Hear the person out; then respond.

Remember: your goal is to be an effective salesperson, not to merely "get your two cents worth in." Always remember that, at this point, your prospect has your "two cents" anyway—right in his or her pocket!

How to Discover What Your Prospect Will Buy

Prepare, in advance, the questions you'll ask. Of course, every prospect is unique and every selling situation requires some variation, but certain basic questions that come up in every interview can be planned in advance. By carefully planning them, you can make sure you cover all bases and that your wording is precise. There is one caution: be careful not to phrase them so they sound canned.

Ask as many open-ended questions as possible. Closed questions that call for a "yes" or "no" answer tend to discourage people from talking, to give only limited information, and they tend to set a negative tone.

During the Probe step, ask primarily open-ended questions that require prospects to tell you how they feel, what they want, or what they think. There is room for "yes" or "no" questions, but be careful not to use too many or to use them incorrectly.

Ask needs-based questions. In the Probe step, you want to do more than get your prospect to talk; you want to find out what he or she needs. Therefore, frame questions that will give you insights into how prospects perceive their needs.

Ask questions that help you identify problems to be solved. Usually there's one overriding problem that needs to be resolved in the prospect's mind—a situation you can understand by asking the right questions. Plus, with proper pre-call planning and strong internal advocacy, you should already know what those problems are.

Ask questions that help you pinpoint the dominant buying motivations. Buying motivations and needs are not always the same. Buying motivations have to do with desires, feelings, tastes, and so on.

Avoid offensive questions or asking questions in an insensitive way. Certain types of questions can offend prospects and cause them to back away from you. Here are some examples of pitfalls to avoid:

- Don't use leading or "setup" questions such as "You do want to make a profit, don't you?" What is the prospect going to say? "No! I don't!"
- Probe; don't pry. Nosey questions can be a real turnoff.
- Be careful about phrasing. For example, instead of asking, "How much can you afford to spend?" you could phrase it more positively: "How much had you planned to invest?"

Ask questions that are easy to answer. Questions that require knowledge the prospect doesn't have can often make him or her feel stupid. For example, asking most consumers, "What's the maximum wattage per channel on your amplifier?" might get you a dumb look for an answer. The smarter you make your prospects feel, the smarter they'll think you are and the more they'll like you.

Use questions to guide the interview and keep the tone positive. Some people love to ramble on and on, but by skillfully using questions you can keep the interview focused and moving in the right direction.

Also, ask questions to which people can easily respond in a positive manner. Studies have shown that most people much prefer to agree than to assert themselves and disagree. Make it easy to say "yes."

Ask—and then listen. The prospect can't talk while you're talking. Besides, you can't learn while you're talking. Don't just get quiet and think up something to say next; instead, listen to every word that prospect says and analyze the words, the tones, and the gestures.

Remember: you can talk people into buying, but you can often listen them into it. Questions are your greatest selling tool.

Avoid These Three Pitfalls

There are three pitfalls that you'll always need to avoid
when asking questions:

- Don't ask a question and then answer it for your prospect.
- Don't interrupt your prospect when he or she is responding to a
  question.
- Don't fail to ask a minimum of three follow-up questions, like "Tell
  me more," then "Could you expand on that?" and finally, "What was
  the result?" when you uncover a real issue that you can help your
  prospect solve with your product or service.

The better you become at asking questions, the easier it will
become for you to sell.

I'm sure you've heard that if you give someone a fish, he or
she eats that day, but if you teach someone to fish, he or she will
eat for a lifetime. Let's teach you how to fish for the right answers
by showing how you can construct just the right questions.

It's All About Solving Challenges

All things being equal, prospects will act most quickly on a purchase decision to alleviate a problem, challenge, difficulty, or
inconvenience they're facing with a current situation, a condition, or a competitive product or service. Ideally, through your
internal advocate and/or your pre-call research you should
know if they're facing a challenge. If that's the case, you should
prepare questions like these in advance:

- How much downtime are you experiencing with your
  equipment? (challenge: downtime)
- How much turnover are you experiencing because of current work conditions? (challenge: turnover)
- How much is this poor service costing you? (challenge:
  poor service)

If you're not able to learn enough about your prospect
before you get face to face, you may have to rely on more general questions like this: "Many of our customers in your busi-

> ## Challenge Identification Questions
> To develop these questions, simply list the single biggest challenge or set of challenges your prospect is facing, such as poor quality. Then develop a question you can ask about that challenge, such as "What level of quality are you receiving?" Now, develop three follow-up questions, such as "What will happen if that continues?" "How long could you put up with that?" and "What needs to be resolved?"

ness have told us that they are trying to solve issues related to fading colors. What has your experience been with this issue?"

How Do Your Features and Benefits Stack Up?

Lots of salespeople have a tendency to believe that their prospects buy features. Do yours? I'll bet they're more likely to buy the benefits that those features deliver. A feature is how it's described technically or constructed (e.g., "It has a triple coating"). The benefit is what it'll do for your customer ("It'll last longer").

> ## Sell Benefits, Not Features
> When you sell benefits, you're focusing on your prospects and their needs, on what's of interest to them. When you sell features, you're focusing on your products or services.
> If a benefit of your product is of no value to your prospects, they certainly don't need the feature no matter what you think of it.

You'll need to learn how to ask benefit-driven questions to determine if your prospect even needs or wants the features that drive the benefit. Here are some examples of benefit-driven questions:

- How important is longer-lasting wear to you? (feature: triple-coated; benefit: lasts longer)
- How long do you normally keep your equipment in operation? (feature: 10-year warranty; benefit: long-term protection)

- What sort of life insurance do you have? (feature: life insurance policy contained with health insurance policy you're selling; benefit: low-cost life insurance)

But think about this for a minute. What if you already knew the answers to these questions *before* you ever got to this point? What if your internal advocate told you about the problems they're having and the benefits they're seeking? Your questions may then be like these.

- Knowing that you keep your equipment for five years, how important is longer-lasting wear to you?
- Understanding that you try to keep your equipment in operation for 10 years, how essential is a 10-year warranty to you?
- It's my understanding that your life insurance has lapsed. What plans, if any, have you made to protect your family?

This scenario, by the way, will be the same for every type of question you'll ask. Here's the secret: the Investigate step will tell you every question to ask before you ever meet with your prospect! Most of the selling occurs in the Investigate and Probe steps. It's that simple.

Feature/Benefit Questions

To learn how to develop feature/benefit questions, list every feature of your product or service on one side of a piece of paper. Then list the corresponding benefit next to it. To do that, simply ask yourself this question, "What does that do for my customer?" For example:

It's painted orange. What does that do for my customer? It's easy to see from a distance.

Now, ask yourself a question relative to that benefit. For example:

How often do you have to find or locate this product from a distance?

Do this with every feature and benefit for every product or service you sell and you'll have more questions than you'll ever need!

Needs-Based Questions

Fundamentally, your prospects will buy something they need, provided, of course, that they really want it. Needs-based questions are perhaps the most basic questions that you'll need to learn how to ask.

In order to master this type of question, you'll need to know the real needs that your product or service fills for your customers. As simple as that sounds, it's not always easy. It's not unusual for salespeople to be so focused on themselves or their products or services that the customer is never a part of the equation.

So, let me ask you a question. What needs do you fill for your customers? Do you really know? Do they buy for financial or personal gain? To solve a problem? Cosmetic reasons? Peace of mind? To make family members happy? There are as many reasons as there are products and services.

Let's use an example. Imagine for a moment that you sell automobiles. More specifically, you sell mid-priced, domestically manufactured vehicles to young families. Among other needs, these families need:

1. A mid-priced, affordable vehicle
2. A vehicle that will carry a family of five (husband, wife, three children)
3. Good gas mileage
4. Minimal maintenance
5. Good trade-in value

How would you have known these needs if you hadn't asked the families the following questions:

1. What type of price range do you have in mind?
2. How many are in your family? How old are your children?
3. How many miles a year do you drive? How important is gas mileage to you?
4. How important is ease of maintenance to you?
5. How long do you plan to keep the vehicle? Do you trade? How important is trade-in value to you?

Needs-Based Questions

Sit down somewhere quiet. Get a legal pad and a pen and get ready to think. List your products or services on a sheet of paper and then, for each one, start to ask yourself this question, "What needs do we fill for our customers with this product or service?" List as many as you can. Don't be surprised if you get stuck at five or six. But, trust me, there are at least 20.

Now, after you list them, ask yourself this question, "What would I have to ask a prospect to find out if each of the needs I've listed mattered to him or her?"

For example, you sell real estate and have listed a high-end, six-bedroom home:

Need that home fulfills:	Question to ask:
Lots of sleeping space	How often do you have out of town guests?
Prestige	Tell me about your business associates.
Swimming pool	How often, if ever, do you entertain outdoors?

Objection-Based Questions

Contemporary selling is far different from old school selling. In the old days, you'd memorize a whole series of canned ways to handle objections. Your goal was to outwit and outmaneuver your prospect.

Today, your goal is different, easier, far less manipulative, and much more straightforward. You need to learn how to ask questions that relate to the most common objections you'll get. Your prospect's answers will tell you one of two things: either you may not get the objections at all or you'll know exactly how to position your product or service in the Apply step in order to deal with the problem in a straightforward and honest way. Either way, you'll be far better off than if you didn't know that the problem was coming.

These are by far the three most common objections salespeople receive:

1. I want to think about it.
2. Your price is too high.
3. I need to talk to my boss.

And as common as these objections are, they usually come out of the blue for the unskilled salesperson.

Let's take a look at just one question you can ask in the Probe step to pre-empt these objections and three possible responses to each:

Objection 1: What type of process do you use for purchases like this and how far along are you on that process?

1. "I like to think about it."
2. "I like to think about things but am prepared to make a decision with 10 days."
3. "I'm making a decision this week."

Objection 2: What type of budget do you have in mind for a project like this?

1. "I'll need to check with our budgeting people to find that out."
2 "We haven't established a budget, we're looking at suppliers like you to get an idea about pricing."
3. "We'll spend between $500 and $1,000 per unit."

Objection 3: Who else, other than you, of course, will be involved in making this decision?

1. "I need to talk to my boss."
2. "I'll be involved, but my boss will make the final call."
3. "I'm making the decision myself."

Do you notice how effective it is to ask the questions in the Probe step and how silly you will look later in the sale if you don't ask the right questions now? In each case, by asking the right questions, no matter what the answer, you'll have somewhere to go with your sales strategy. If you do not ask the questions soon enough, you will face insurmountable objections later!

Think Negatively

List the most common objections you hear about your product or service and then develop a question or two that you ask in the Probe step to tell you exactly how to handle each one most effectively.

Here are two examples:

Objection: Your competitor has better delivery.

Probe question: How familiar are you with our new delivery policy?

Objection: We only deal with local vendors.

Probe question: How familiar are you with our latest digital technology that allows us to be everywhere in just seconds?

14 Winning Questions

Everyone likes things to be easy. That probably includes you, too. So, to achieve that goal, let's take a look at 14 questions that have proven to be winners over the years in hundreds of industries and with tens of thousands of salespeople. Think of them as silver bullets for your sales gun.

Please feel free to copy these questions and use them over and over again. They'll serve you well no matter what you sell. However, here's a tip. Combine them with the questions we've taught you how to develop and you'll be a real sales champion.

- What are some of the major challenges within your business in the past 12 months?
- What impact have these had on your profits/morale/success?
- What, if anything, is something you would never want to see changed?
- What do you like most about your current supplier?
- What kind of time frame are you working within?
- What kind of a budget range do you have in mind?
- What have you seen that's particularly appealed to you?
- What process do you use to make this type of decision?
- Who else, other than you, of course, is involved in this decision?

- If you could change anything about your current situation, what would it be?
- What is the single thing that's most important to you about this decision?
- If we were able to solve your problem, what would this mean to your organization?
- What would solving your problem mean to you personally?

Prepare Completely Before You Continue

This secret is worth its weight in gold to you. Remember the IMPACT Selling System rule that says you should never go to a step until you have completed the previous step?

This rule is especially true in the Probe step. Here's why. Far too many salespeople will uncover a benefit or two, a problem they can solve, or a need that they can fill and immediately proceed to the Apply step. Don't do that! Never go into a gunfight with a half-loaded gun. You must absolutely, positively uncover as many needs, problems, benefits, answers, solutions, or issues that you can solve as humanly possible. Before you even think about leaving the Probe step and moving on, you need to load your gun completely.

It's All in the Stars
Each time you ask a question and uncover a specific issue you can solve, place a star or asterisk next to that question. When you have five to seven stars or asterisks, you'll be in a position to move on, but not until then. Don't give in to temptation ... or you'll be going forward with a half-empty gun!

Remember that you've been recording your answers on your notepad or on a prepared sheet of questions you have developed. As you start to finalize the Probe step, you'll now issue a *summary statement*. This is simply a reflective process where you are clarifying and summing up for your prospect what he or she has told you.

John and Sam

John sells property insurance. At the end of the Probe, he told his prospect, "What I understood you to say is that you'd like to insure the contents at 25% more value, you're very concerned about your collectibles, and you're not comfortable with your current terms of coverage. You'd also like us to review your paperwork to make sure you have filled it out correctly. Is that right?"

His prospect's response, "Yes, that's correct. But I'd also like to talk to you about some additional coverage for our new beach house."

Here's how Sam, his competitor, handled the same prospect:

"I can help you with contents. But let me tell you about the new policy I can sell you for your house that I've heard you got at the beach. You're really going to like it. I know I can get you the best rates, too. Let me show you how we can do that!"

John summarizes what he heard the prospect tell him, which opens the door to meeting this person's needs. Sam launches into a product selling spiel that may seem more in his best interest than his prospect's.

The Most Powerful Word You Can Use

Professionals sell advice. The only way to give useful, valuable advice is to ask the right questions. Then you need to make a strong recommendation. Therefore, the most powerful word you can use is "recommend." Here's exactly how to use it.

Issue a summary statement once you understand what your prospect is looking for in terms of a solution or resolution for his or her problem. For example, "I understand you're looking for something that we have in stock, is within your price range, and has a three-year warranty." Then determine if your understanding is correct by asking, "Is that correct?" When you get a positive response, you simply say, "Based on what you're after, I'm going to recommend _____," filling in the blank with the product, service, or solution you're recommending—the one that fits your prospect's requirement perfectly!

The Probe step is, fundamentally, the most critical part of the face-to-face sale. You need to invest most of your face-to-face time here. Don't be tempted to leave it too soon or to be premature in assuming you know exactly what, when, how, and

Are You Missing Anything?

What if your prospect's answer is something like this? "No, that's not what I meant. What I meant is ...."

No problem. Simply ask your prospect this question, "Is there anything else I missed?" You're returning to the Probe step in order to identify anything that you've misunderstood or to discover if there's anything else that needs to be covered. Once you're sure your prospect has explained his or her situation, issue a revised summary statement that captures the new information.

under what conditions and circumstances your prospect will buy your product or service. Proceed only when you are 100% positive that the recommendation you'll make is the one they'll accept. It's really that easy. Don't make it any more difficult.

Checklist for Chapter 8

❏ The fatal flaw in selling is to be so focused on what you want to have happen that you lose sight of what the prospect wants to have happen. The fatal flaw can turn all of your positioning, prospecting, pre-call planning and meeting efforts into failure.

❏ You can ask the right questions and still get nowhere if you don't have the basic, fundamental skills of listening. To sell well, you must be a good active listener.

❏ All things being equal, prospects will act most quickly on a purchase decision to alleviate a problem, challenge, difficulty, or inconvenience they're facing with a current situation, a condition, or a competitive product.

❏ A feature is how your product is described technically or constructed. The benefit is what it'll do for your customer.

❏ Ask benefit-driven questions to determine if your prospect even needs or wants the features that drive the benefit.

❏ Ask questions that relate to the most common objections you'll get. You may not get the objections at all or the answers will indicate exactly how to position your product or service in the Apply step in order to deal with the problem in a straightforward and honest way.

❏ Far too many salespeople will uncover a benefit or two, a problem they can solve, or a need that they can fill and immediately proceed to the Apply step. Don't do that!

❏ Professionals sell advice. The only way to give useful, valuable advice is to ask the right questions. Then make a strong recommendation. The most powerful word you can use is "recommend."

❏ The Probe step is the most critical part of the face-to-face sale.

The Apply Step: Making Your Product or Service Solve Problems

A pply: To show the prospect precisely *how* your recommended product or service meets his or her specific needs.
To make the correct recommendation in such a way that the
prospect sees, feels, and experiences the *application* of the
product or service to solve his or her problem or fill his or her
specific need.

Application-Based Selling vs. Demonstration-Based Selling

There's a big difference between simply presenting your product
or service to a prospect and carefully recommending your product or service as something that solves a specific problem, fills
an exact want, satisfies a stated need, or provides a unique
answer that the prospect is seeking. In the final analysis, the
only reason your prospect would buy anything from you is if he
or she can see that what you offer is more valuable than simply

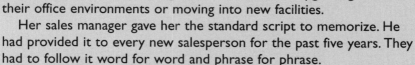

It's More Than Just the Picture

Jodi was a new salesperson with her company. Her job was selling full-color prints to organizations that were upgrading their office environments or moving into new facilities.

Her sales manager gave her the standard script to memorize. He had provided it to every new salesperson for the past five years. They had to follow it word for word and phrase for phrase.

Armed with her memorized presentation, Jodi went to work, and she sold nothing for three months. Not one single print. Then she changed her tactics. She started going "off the script" and presenting her products based on the answers to the questions she asked. If color was an issue, she stressed color. If size was important, she addressed size. If delivery time would make the difference, she stressed delivery.

Her sales suddenly skyrocketed. What was the difference?

doing nothing or purchasing from your competitor.

Four Pointers That Guarantee Sales

Here are four suggestions to guide you in making the Apply step work.

Pointer 1: Choose Only the Most Appropriate Product or Service

As simple as it sounds, choosing the right product or service to recommend to your prospect is a vital part of the Apply step. Yet it is also one of the most troublesome, for two big reasons.

First, salespeople often skip right over the Probe step and go immediately into a generic product demonstration. After all, they reason, there's no need to waste time. The prospect generally knows what he or she wants and they can show other products or benefits later, right? Wrong!

A photocopier salesman once confessed to me that he learned a valuable lesson by blowing a sale he could have made. A prospect's secretary called and said her boss wanted to see a copier that day, so Tony, the salesperson, set up an appointment for late that afternoon.

He was so excited that he actually threw the top-of-the-line model into his employer's delivery truck and drove 50 miles to make the standard demo. He allowed plenty of time to set up, because the model he chose could run colors, collate thousands of pages, and do everything but make coffee.

"I don't need all that stuff," the prospect said as soon as he saw the machine. "We never do colors and we don't have any use for collating. All I want is a machine that will give me top-quality prints of single pages and spit them out in a hurry." He didn't even ask the price.

When Tony promised to be back the next morning with the right machine, the man said he was going out of town that night and suggested that he call for an appointment "next week." You can guess what happened next. When Tony called to make an appointment, he learned that his prospect had bought a competitor's product at a higher price than his basic copier would have cost.

Very often you get only one good shot at properly demonstrating your product or service. Even if you get a second chance, anything you'll show then is anticlimactic. Downgrading can be embarrassing for the client and upgrading can be tough for you. The only way to be really sure what to recommend is to probe thoroughly until you are certain about your prospect's wants and needs.

Second, salespeople often show the wrong product because they choose what to recommend based on their own interests, not on the prospect's desires.

Contests Can Hurt
One of the problems with sales contests is that they will often encourage salespeople to show one product to every prospect because that's what their employer is pushing at the moment. As a consequence, they'll walk out with no order rather than selling something else.

Smart professional salespeople know that the right choice of product or service to show is always the one that the prospect is most likely to buy.

Pointer 2: Tailor the Presentation to the Prospect's Needs and Wants

When presenting your products or service, there are four possible focal points:

1. You can focus on the product or service itself, which is what most salespeople do. They love to talk about all the features and variations.
2. You can focus on the organization you represent and talk about its reputation for service, dependability, and fair prices.
3. You can focus attention on yourself by noting that if you sell 200 widgets this week, you'll win a free trip to Bermuda.
4. You can focus on the prospect—what he or she wants or needs and what he or she will gain by buying your product or service.

Let me tell you a little secret: most prospects could not care less about the first three, but if you really hit on number four, you have a good chance of closing a sale. If you want to add more "sell" to your show and tell, get very personal with it.

Pointer 3: Give the Prospects a Show He or She Will Never Forget

The "show" we're talking about here is not the face-to-face version of a carefully scripted and rehearsed infomercial and it is not a piece of sales improv theater. Let me explain.

Canned demonstrations are like a straitjacket—they restrict your ability to tailor your presentation to the prospect's needs and desires. However, that doesn't mean that you need to go to the opposite extreme and slither through a completely spontaneous demonstration, either.

Actually, the application-based approach to presenting your product or service calls for harder work than a canned presentation. It means that you have to know everything about every product or service in your lineup—and you have to know it so well you can present any product or service with equal enthusiasm and force in any sequence. And that's a big order!

Pointer 4: Involve Your Prospect from the Word "Go"

A friend of mine once told me he had decided to buy a certain expensive brand of automobile and went to a dealer's showroom to take a test drive.

"The salesperson acted as if I were going to hurt his car," my friend recalled. "Every time I tried to touch anything on the instrument panel, he'd almost slap my hands. His attitude seemed to be 'You do the paying and leave the driving to us.'"

"Did you buy it?" I asked.

"Sure, I bought a car just like the one I'd been shown—but not from him," he said wryly. "I went to another dealership and bought it from a salesman who put me in the driver's seat all the way."

Getting prospects involved in the process is a much more powerful way to help them experience the transfer of ownership than a contractual agreement. You've got a much better chance to make the sale if you help the prospect feel like he or she is already enjoying the benefits of your product or service.

Real estate salespeople, for example, know that clients must experience psychological ownership of a property before they will sign a purchase agreement. Thus, they usually insist that the selling family not be at home when they show the property to a prospective buyer. They know that few families will come in and "take over" psychological ownership of a home from another family.

Some of the real pros I know in real estate actively

> **TRICKS OF THE TRADE**
>
> ## Get Your Prospects Involved
>
> Do everything in your power to involve your prospects actively. Don't sit across from them; sit next to them. Let them feel, touch, use, and experience your product. Allow them to compute figures on a calculator, run equipment, and become comfortable and familiar with what you're showing them. Fearful prospects buy nothing. Confused ones don't, either. Remove fear and confusion with involvement.

try to involve their prospects in planning what they will do to change the décor and even where they will put their furniture. It helps them to see themselves actually living in the house.

How to Apply the Principles Behind Application-Based Selling

Application Principle 1: The transfer of ownership must occur in a prospect's mind before he or she will sign on any dotted line!

This is all about the mental transfer that can occur only when you actively involve your prospect and enable him or her to experience using whatever you are selling. Remember: selling is definitely a hands-on activity—especially when it comes to your prospect's hands.

Application Principle 2: All sales degenerate into a struggle over price in the absence of a value interpreter.

> ### Andy the Art Broker
> *Tricks of the Trade*
>
> Andy, a successful, high-end art broker, won't *allow* anyone to purchase a painting from him unless he delivers it to the customers' home or office and has it hung exactly where they're going to place it for at least two days. The result? About an 80% closure rate! Plus he always sells more paintings as his customers find other places and ways to upgrade their décor. Why is that? He brings other paintings with him and hangs those as well in other areas!

What does this mean? Simply this. If your prospect is constantly telling you that he or she can get an equal or better price somewhere else, you have failed to create sufficient value for your product or service. Your prospect is telling you that he or she doesn't see sufficient value to offset the price. As a consequence, the prospect has one single goal—to get you to lower your price! More about that in a minute.

But first, what is value? It can be explained very easily, through the formula shown in Figure 9-1.

Value equals perceived benefits over price and perceived emotional cost. Here's how it works. If your prospect believes

$$V = \frac{PB \uparrow}{PP/PEC \downarrow}$$

Figure 9-1. Formula for value, positive

that the benefits that he or she will receive by purchasing your product or service are greater than what he or she will pay for it (price) and any difficulties with terms, conditions, transition, etc. (perceived emotional cost), your prospect sees value. If this occurs, you'll have no problem with price.

> **Key Term**
>
> **Perceived emotional cost** The amount of time, risk, change, or commitment that your prospect will have to invest in owning or using your product or service.
>
> Perception is important here. That's because it's still true that perception is reality. You must create the perception of value that will offset the actual price and perceived emotional cost of your offering.

Figure 9-2.

However, if the opposite occurs, you'll have problems. That looks like

$$V = \frac{PB \downarrow}{PP/PEC \uparrow}$$

Figure 9-2. Formula for value, negative

In this case, your prospect feels that the benefits he or she will receive from your product or service are not sufficient to justify the price and perceived emotional cost. The benefits just are not worth the financial and psychological investment.

How do you solve this challenge? It's really simple. Invest time in the Probe step asking lots of questions relative to benefits your prospect wants. Invest a lot of time asking about the problems he or she wants to eliminate. Ask about the needs to be satisfied. Ask the prospect about risks, problems and challenges, and hassles he or she wants to avoid and issues that are important to him or her.

Then, in the Apply step, you simply address the benefits relative to perceived emotional costs. Present your price only after you have created the right picture of value.

Application Principle 3: All benefits are equal until someone points out the difference.

Smart salespeople never assume anything. And you need to do the same thing. Just because your product has a handle doesn't mean that your prospect even knows it's a handle! Plus, you probably need to show your prospect how much easier your product is to carry. In fact, if you're really smart,

---

Why Roger Is Number One

Roger sells high-end automobiles. He recently worked with a couple who told him the following in the Probe step:

- They wanted a strong warranty, dependability, a good trade-in value, and a specific gold-colored model that had to be in stock. Also, the reputation of the service department was essential.
- They didn't want to take the car in for service, didn't want to finance through a bank, and wanted a dedicated technician to work on their car.

Here's how Roger handled it. He told them about the warranty and its strengths (benefit), stated that dependability was a watchword for the car he recommended (benefit), explained that the car had a tradition of strong trade-in value (benefit), showed them the exact gold-colored car that was in stock (benefit), and allowed them to tour the service department and read the plaques and letters posted from satisfied customers (benefit).

He then explained the dealer's valet program for service (emotional cost savings), presented the manufacturer's finance program as an alternative to the bank (emotional cost savings), and introduced them to Mike, the technician who would be taking care of their new car (emotional cost savings). Then, and only then, did he deal with the price of the car.

Had Roger created value? Yes. Did he have much problem with price? No. And he sold the car. By the way, he's been the top salesperson at his dealership for the past five years. Do you know why?

How Bob Booted the Sale

Bob was a consultant. He delivered Personal Effectiveness and Peak Performance seminars for corporate clients. As part of his services, he regularly went into the clients' facilities and conducted a needs analysis to determine the exact parameters for designing their specific program.

But Bob had gotten a little sloppy recently, even arrogant. He believed that everyone should buy from him because his programs were so good. So, when trying to sell a prospect a series of seminars, he failed to mention that he provided a needs analysis as part of his services.

Then, when he called to confirm that his prospect was ready to start the training program, he learned that the prospect had decided to work with a competitor. When he asked why, the prospect said it was because the competitor would conduct a needs analysis before the training.

"But," Bob responded, "I do, too."

"But," the prospect responded, "you never told us."

How did Bob lose this valuable account? What should he have done? What will he be sure to do next time?

you'll let your prospect actually tote it around, to feel how much easier it is to carry than your competitor's product.

Never assume that your prospect understands the benefit that a feature offers. Always point it out. Also, be sure to show every benefit as if it's exclusive with your product or service. Why? Because if your competitors fail to mention their benefit, yours will become an exclusive! Again, perception is reality.

Application Principle 4: All benefits are intangible until someone makes them tangible—and all intangible benefits can be made tangible.

Think about your travel agent. How attractive would a trip to an exotic island be without pictures? Simply discussing something is not enough. Your prospects need to see tangible evidence of what your product or service will offer. This is the real role that your sales aids and tools play—to help you tell your

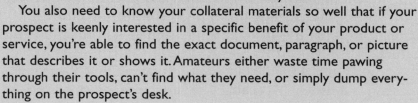

It's All About Organization

Smart salespeople will assemble their briefcase or organize themselves so that they can retrieve or easily locate the precise sales aid at the exact, correct moment they need it.

You also need to know your collateral materials so well that if your prospect is keenly interested in a specific benefit of your product or service, you're able to find the exact document, paragraph, or picture that describes it or shows it. Amateurs either waste time pawing through their tools, can't find what they need, or simply dump everything on the prospect's desk.

"benefits story"… and not to serve as a means for presenting your product or service. And there's a big difference.

Four Proven Ways to Make a Better Presentation

Here are four tips you'll need to learn and apply in order to be able to present your product or service with the power that it deserves.

Tip 1: Avoid Making Price an Issue

Interestingly, studies show that the typical salesperson is a lot more concerned about price than is the typical customer.

Amateur salespeople seem to love to talk about price. They compare one product with another on the basis of costs, they talk incessantly about the size of discounts they can give, and they boast about having a lower price than their competitors.

Unfortunately, all that does is serve to remind the prospect of how much the product is going to cost. Even if the prospect is not overly concerned about price at the beginning of the sales interview, he or she will become more and more attuned to it the more you talk about it.

Smart salespeople handle price as if it were a minor consideration. Of course, when the prospect makes it an issue, they deal with it effectively. But even then, they try to minimize its importance. The next three tips will show you how smart salespeople minimize the price and perceived emotional cost factors.

Tip 2: Focus on Benefits, Not Features or Price

Do you recall our discussion in the Probe step about the difference between a feature and a benefit? A *feature* is an attribute of a product or service—some quality that makes it attractive. A *benefit* is an advantage that a particular feature provides. Benefits are what a given customer will derive from a particular feature.

For example, a handle on the top is a feature, but ease of handling is a benefit. Availability of service nationwide is a feature, but convenience to the customer is the benefit. An overdrive transmission is a feature, but better gas mileage is the benefit the customer will derive from ownership.

The best way to answer your prospect's most important question is to focus all your attention on the benefits the person will derive from using your product or service. This whole discussion may sound rather basic, but the difference in impact is enormous. Think about this.

All values are considered equal until someone points out the difference!

Remember: the smart salesperson never assumes that any fool can see that a handle on the top makes a product easier to carry. He or she *shows* how much easier it is to carry. In fact, really smart professionals will let the prospect *feel* how much easier it is to carry!

Never assume that a prospect understands the benefit a feature offers. Always point it out. What's more, sell every benefit as if it were the greatest thing since sliced bread. The more benefits you apply to the prospect's needs or wants, the more often you show the prospect what he or she will get from buying the product or service.

Tip 3: Focus on Value—and Then Work to Deliver It

Showing your prospect the benefits of ownership is the way you create value; in fact, it's the only way you have to create value. The more value you create, the more desirable the product or service becomes to the prospect and the less important price or cost becomes.

But go beyond simply verbalizing those benefits and the value. Work hard to make your prospect feel them. With a little ingenuity, you can usually get your prospect to verbalize those values to you in his or her own words. Only then will you know for sure that your prospect has accepted the values you've offered.

Tip 4: Relate Every Benefit to Value

One way you can focus attention on value is to relate it to every benefit.

The dictionary says that value is "worth in money" and that what gives something its value is its "desirability" to the person who values it. So your task is to translate every benefit of every feature into a tangible value— something the prospect desires. Create enough desirability and you've got yourself a sale.

Many salespeople make a big deal of the difference between "tangible" value and "intangible" value. A tangible value is one you can see, hear, touch, taste, or smell. An intangible value has more to do with emotions, logic, or some unseen factor.

> ### The Fire Truck and the Insurance Policy
>
> Sal sells fire trucks to municipalities. He regularly demonstrates the velocity of hoses, varied alarm signals, transmission durability, and length of service for the trucks he sells.
>
> Ann sells health insurance. Ann stresses peace of mind, minimizing risk, and the importance of family security.
>
> Which one of these salespeople stresses tangible benefits? Intangible ones?
>
> Could Ann make her benefits tangible? Could she show actual hospital bills and coverage her company has provided? Could Sal show intangible benefits, that the fire trucks he sells provide peace of mind and a sense of well-being?

How to Present Your Price and Get It

There is no issue that nags salespeople more than this one. Exactly when and how do you present price?

The "when" is easy. You present it as late as you possibly can in your sales presentation. You'll want to present your price only after you're able to create perceived benefits that far exceed price and perceived emotional cost. Present it only after you have been able to create sufficient value for your offering.

Your prospects are eagerly and appropriately interested in price. And they should be. However, your goal is to avoid offering it prematurely. Your goal should be to defer price discussions as long as you possibly can. Your purpose is to present your product or service in a light that focuses primarily on the benefits and elimination of problems instead of price.

Your prospect may ask you the price of your product or service before you've created sufficient value for it. Quite often, the premature price question will come up in the Meet step. You'll need to know exactly how to deal with that question easily and quickly.

Smart salespeople know to answer premature price questions with a response that goes something like this:

> *I understand that price is important. And it should be. We've got a full range of prices, depending upon options, choices, volume, and a lot of other factors. What I'd like to do is to make sure that this is the exact product, with the right features, that is exactly right for you. Then I'll give you the price right to the penny. Does that make sense?*

This strategy of deferring the inevitable question will be successful for several reasons. First, it shows you're listening. Second, it shows that you're concerned about recommending the most effective solution for the prospect. Third, it communicates that you'll give the exact price. Finally, it gives the prospect a chance to allow you to go ahead without prematurely disclosing your price. And they'll allow you to do so 99% of the time!

Price Pitfalls

When presenting your price, you'll always want to present it within the structure of benefits. You'll never want to fall prey to the temptation to simply say, "It costs X dollars."

There are several other things you'll want to avoid when presenting your price. Let's talk about them.

Avoid Modifiers

Don't ever say things like "our regular price is ..." or "our standard price is ..." or "our suggested retail price is ...." Why not? Look at it from the point of view of your prospect. If someone said to you, "Our list price is ...," what do you expect to come next? Here it is: "But for you, the price will be a lot less!" Mention "regular price" or "standard price" or "suggested retail price" and you'll be setting yourself up for that very same expectation. And when you don't meet that expectation, your prospect will either object to your price, ask for an exception to it, seek another option, or simply fail to buy.

Avoid Setting Yourself up for Failure

One of the most common price presentation errors is to set yourself up for guaranteed failure by making statements like these: "We really want your business, so tell me, where do we need to be on price?" or "What price point do we need to meet in order to get your business?"

That is not selling. It's begging. And you're not a beggar. You're a professional salesperson.

Managing Price-Cutting Attempts

No matter how effectively or strongly you present your price, expect your prospects to seek a better price, improved terms, more for their money, or additional benefits.

Why is that? There are lots of reasons. For one, we all want the best deal. Also, there are lots of competitors in any industry who are more than willing to drop their price in order to get the business. It's a buyer's market in segments that are highly competitive and crowded.

The most important thing to remember is that your success in sales will be driven by two essential factors—margin and volume. Smart salespeople understand that they are expected to sell their products or services at a profit. They're not tempted to discount, give things away, or lose money on transactions. The

Presenting Your Price with Confidence

TRICKS OF THE TRADE Here's how Roger, the luxury car salesperson, presented the price of the high-end, expensive vehicle to his two prospects.

"Let me tell you everything that goes with this vehicle. You'll receive the full, 100%, three-year warranty and the heavier suspension and the knowledge that this vehicle has proven its dependability for over 20 years, we can have it ready for you this morning, it's in the exact gold color you want, and we can have Mike get it ready and assign him as your dedicated technician. I've already shown you the five-year performance in terms of trade-in value. You can get all of this for only a $5,000 down payment and $900 per month for 60 months. But here's the great part. You will be able to handle all of the financial paperwork here at the dealership, rather than requiring you to go to the bank, and we can set up our free valet service today so you won't have to drop your vehicle off for servicing. How does that sound?"

Roger first reviewed all of the benefits his prospects wanted, in order. He then presented the price. He ended by mentioning the perceived emotional costs that his prospects wanted to avoid. The result? He "stacked" the price between benefits and perceived emotional costs, so the perception of price is significantly diminished and the perception of value is enhanced. That's how to present price!

really smart ones also get into the groove of consistently selling their products or services at significant margins.

It's About the Math

To deal with price-cutting attempts, you simply need to understand how to use addition, multiplication, or subtraction. Here's how that works. When your prospect says, "Your price is too high" (which is, by the way, the phrase any salesperson anywhere in the world hears more than any other), you need to first acknowledge his or her response.

You can do that in several ways. For example, you should first agree by saying, "Perhaps it is." You may want to ask, "What is it about the price that concerns you?" The response? "It's the amount. It's too high. That's what I told you!" However, your prospect might have a different response, like "I'll have trouble getting the others to agree to this price" or "Could you explain to me how you arrived at that price?"

Never Compare an Apple to an Apple ... Compare It to a Pear

Your prospects will often want to "compare an apple to an apple." Your goal is to separate your offering from every competitor's offering so that it's impossible to do that. An apple is not a pear.

Let's take a look at Roger again. He could have differentiated his $59,000 vehicle even further by pointing out additional benefits that differentiated it from the competition—additional safety features, computer-driven mini-motors, the owners membership club, safety clinics, the action transition team, clinics that show new buyers how to care for their vehicle better, etc.

Never allow prospects to compare your product or service item for item, benefit by benefit, or feature by feature to any other competitive product. If you don't do that, you'll be allowing yourself and your product or service to become a commodity—and you don't ever want to do that.

Now, you start to become a mathematician. Here are your options:

"Let me tell you why our price is where it is."

Repeat each of the benefits you provide and the emotional costs you will save them (addition). *or*

"Let me explain to you how each of the things we've discussed will help you."

Expand and repeat the benefits they'll receive and the emotional relief you'll provide them (multiplication).

"We can work to give you a better price. But to do that, we'll have to remove some of the components we've discussed. Which would you like to eliminate?"

Your prospect will likely not want to remove or reduce any of the benefits you've provided. Therefore, this last option is your last resort. However, salespeople are shocked when they use this last option (subtraction)—because prospect after prospect will find a way to find the money for the product or service!

Addition Listing each benefit you provide and each perceived emotional cost you remove.

Multiplication Expanding and explaining the value that your prospect will receive from each benefit you'll provide and perceived emotional cost you remove.

Subtraction Offering to remove certain valuable components of your offer in order to reduce your price to an acceptable level. This is your last option.

It's All About Feedback

During the Apply step, you'll need to be sure to determine that the prospect hears your message and that your presentation is on target. Asking for the prospect's reactions and feelings does three very important things for you.

It lets you know where you stand. You might discover that you can close the sale if you can clear up one or two issues. You might also discover that there are several conditions to be met before you can wrap it up. Or you might discover that you can't make the sale under any conditions. At least you'll know what you need to do—even if it's to pack up and move on.

You enable prospects to admit to themselves how they feel and commit to you on how they'll act. By verbalizing their feelings, they can often clarify things for themselves. You'll probably have smoother sailing once your clients can hear their own voices saying, "I like it!"

It enables you to reinforce positive feelings and clear up any misconceptions prospects may have. By getting their reactions, you will see if you've communicated what you'd intended. If they understand what you've said and feel positive about it, you can reinforce the values you've created and help them move toward psychological ownership. On the other hand, you might discover they've misunderstood some point you've made. If so, you can clear it up before you move on.

Some Sample Feedback Questions

Have you ever had a conversation with someone who never asked you your reactions, level of understanding, or degree of agreement with what he or she had been saying? You need to be sure that you don't do this when presenting your product or service. Let's take a look at some ways for you to get feedback from your prospects and determine exactly how they are hearing, understanding, and agreeing with your presentation. For example:

- How does this look?
- Does this make sense?
- Does this look like something you could use?
- How are we doing so far?
- What do you think?
- Do you feel this could help you?
- Do you understand everything so far?
- Can you see yourself using this?
- Does this look like what you've been looking for?
- Are we on target?

Always remember that there is a big difference between application-based selling and demonstration-based selling. One allows you to create value, stack benefits, reduce perceived emotional costs, and make a presentation that is 100% on target to address your prospect's most pressing needs or situation. The other is inflexible and leads to nothing but price problems. Avoid it at all costs.

Where Do You Go?

In order to determine if your presentation is on target, you need to solicit your prospects' reactions to what they see, hear, and understand. Their answer will give you a clear picture of how you're doing.

If you get a response from your prospect like "I don't understand what you said" or "I don't agree with that," don't panic. Simply ask what he or she doesn't understand or doesn't agree with and be sure there's no other problem ("Is there anything else you don't understand?" or "Is there anything else you don't agree with?"). Now simply rephrase what your prospect didn't understand into words he or she can understand or restate your position on the issue that he or she disagreed with. It really is as simple as that—and that easy, too.

Checklist for Chapter 9

❏ There's a big difference between simply presenting your product or service to a prospect and carefully recommending your product or service as something that provides what your prospect wants.

❏ Four actions guarantee sales:
1. Choose only the most appropriate product or service.
2. Tailor the presentation to your prospect's needs and wants.
3. Give a show your prospect will never forget.
4. Involve your prospect from the word "go."

❏ There are four principles behind application-based selling:
1. The transfer of ownership must occur in a prospect's mind before he or she will sign on any dotted line!
2. All sales degenerate into a struggle over price in the absence of a value interpreter.
3. All benefits are equal until someone points out the difference.
4. All benefits are intangible until someone makes them tangible—and all intangible benefits can be made tangible.

❏ To make a better presentation:
1. Avoid making price an issue.
2. Focus on benefits, not features or price.
3. Focus on value—and then work to deliver it.
4. Relate every benefit to value.

❏ Present price as late as possible in your sales presentation, only after you've created perceived benefits that far exceed price and perceived emotional cost. Then, present it within the structure of benefits.

❏ No matter how effectively or strongly you present your price, expect your prospects to seek a better price, improved terms, more for their money, or additional benefits.

❏ Success in sales is driven by margin and volume. Smart salespeople are not tempted to discount, give things away, or lose money on transactions.

❏ To deal with price-cutting attempts, you simply need to understand how to use addition, multiplication, or subtraction.

❏ Asking for the prospect's reactions and feelings does three very important things for you:
1. It lets you know where you stand.
2. You enable prospects to admit to themselves how they feel and commit to you on how they'll act.
3. It enables you to reinforce positive feelings and clear up any misconceptions prospects may have.

The Convince Step: Making Your Prospect Believe

When people believe something enough, they'll take action on it. In addition, prospects expect a salesperson to make claims for their product or service. But they are impressed when someone else does … and when they have the opportunity to actually experience the claims and enjoy the successes promised to them. Before buying a product or a service, a prospect must believe what he or she hears and feels about that product or service.

Sales <u>Is</u> a Worthy Profession

It's an unfortunate reality that there are some salespeople whose lack of credibility places lots of other salespeople in a bad light. Don't be surprised if you read polls that place salespeople very low in terms of believability or honesty.

But you don't need to apologize for those other people. You also don't need to feel as if you should find another profession. What you do need to do is understand the view that is held toward salespeople and do something about it to ensure that the view doesn't lose sales for you.

That's precisely why the Convince step is so critical to your sales success. Never, ever short-change, skip, or forget this step. To do so is to set yourself up for failure and disappointment.

> **Integrity** Ensuring that whatever you say, believe, or commit to do will be consistent with your highest beliefs, that your promises and your actions are totally congruent.

Key Term

What People Believe Enough, They Act Upon

It's not unusual to read polls that show that salespeople rank among the lowest of all professionals in credibility. There's an old joke:

Do you know how you can always tell when a salesman is lying?

No.

If he waves both arms in the air, he may be telling you the truth. If he jumps all over the place and won't look you in the eye, he still may be telling you the truth. But if he ever opens his mouth, he's lying!

How deserved the reputation for dishonesty among salespeople may be is a matter of opinion, but the important fact we all have to face is that it is real. What makes it such a crucial fact is that your livelihood depends upon how much people believe what you say.

A second important piece of reality is that each prospect has his or her own belief system against which all other beliefs are measured. And, never forget, prospects will do what they want to do or, at least, what they believe is best for them.

The challenge can be stated as a principle:

Convince Principle 1: What people believe strongly enough, they act upon!

If people believe strongly enough that what you are selling will be worth more to them than the money you're asking for it, they'll buy it, and if they don't, they won't! It's that simple.

If you are going to make a great living at selling, your only choice is to find ways to cut through all the mistrust and conflicting values to convince your prospects that what you say is true and that the benefits you offer outweigh the price you are asking.

That's a big order, but thousands of truly professional salespeople do it every day. You can, too. Let's take a look at exactly how you can *consistently* convince prospects of the value of your product or service—time after time, day after day. There are basically four actions you can take in the Convince step to set the stage for your prospects to buy:

1. You can prove your claims.
2. You can bring your own witnesses.
3. You can justify your price.
4. You can relieve the prospects' fear of buying.

Let's explore them one at a time.

Prove Your Claims

It might damage your ego, but it will certainly help your bank account to assume that most prospects will not believe anything you say unless you prove it to them. In all fairness, you really must admit that most of your prospects have a right to be skeptical about our claims for several reasons.

First, you stand to gain something if they believe you. Many, many years ago, Secretary of State Henry Kissinger told about a reaction he once got from the late Chairman Mao Tse-tung of China.

"What do you want from us?" Mao asked bluntly.

"We don't want anything but your friendship," Kissinger replied.

"If you want nothing, you shouldn't be here; and if I wanted nothing, I wouldn't have invited you here, so let's get down to business," said the crafty old chairman.

Today's alert prospects feel the same way. They know that you stand to gain something if they buy, so they'll balance everything you say against that fact.

Second, they've been lied to before. The Federal Trade Commission's "truth in advertising" rules have made it harder for the unscrupulous to get away with lying, but a person who wants badly enough to get around them can stretch the truth enough that it is essentially a lie. If you doubt that, all you have to do is think about your own experiences in buying.

Third, people have become jaded by oversell. By the time the average person reaches adulthood, he or she will have seen more than a million television commercials and heard nearly as many radio spots promising everything from robust health and instant wealth to perpetual happiness. To survive, most people have developed very effective mental tune-out devices that just filter out any promise they question.

These and other factors make the Convince step absolutely crucial to your selling success. You have to prove every claim you make about your product or service, about your company, and about yourself.

Here are some ways you can do it.

Claim Prover 1: Never Make a Claim You Can't Back Up with Facts

Personal and professional integrity are absolutely essential to successful selling in today's marketplace. Honesty is vital: mak-

---

Never Presume Anything!

Has a salesperson ever misrepresented something to you? Has someone you know ever told you about a situation where a salesperson misrepresented something to him or her?

How did you feel? How did your friend or family member feel? What is your opinion of the salesperson who was less than honest? Do you think that your prospects have had a similar experience? If so, do you think they may lump you in with the salespeople who are less than honorable?

Never presume anything! Presume that your prospects will never believe anything you say unless it's totally verified by something you can show them or do for them or they can experience the validity of your claims.

ing even one false claim will cost you more sales than it will gain for you.

But there's another issue that is equally important. It's not enough for *you* to believe that a claim is true; you must be able to back it up with proof your prospect will accept.

Let's take a look at a principle that can help you enormously in building credibility:

Convince Principle 2: It makes little difference what you believe is true, unless you can prove it to your prospect.

It's as simple as this: one claim proved is worth 100 claims only made and one false claim discovered can do more damage than a truckload of claims proved.

Claim Prover 2: If You Can Prove It, Show Your Evidence

It's important that you actively back up every claim you make, especially those that sound too good to be true.

The smart salesperson frequently offers supporting data, relevant documents, and tangible evidence to prove every claim he or she makes. And, since you can never really know which prospects will doubt which claims, the safest route is to prove them all.

> **MISTAKE PROOFING**
>
> ### It's Too Good to Be True
>
> The more dramatic and outstanding the claim, the more proof it usually requires. If you claim your gadget can triple gas mileage, you'd better plan to show a lot of evidence to back it up.
>
> Second, constantly test to make sure you've given enough evidence for each claim. Always err on the side of caution and have as much testimonial evidence as possible.

Claim Prover 3: Reinforce All Claims Visually

"A picture is worth a thousand words" is an ancient truth. The reason most people believe that statement is because it has proven true in their own experience. What that means to you is that prospects will much more easily believe and remember what you *show* them than what you only *tell* them.

Simple graphic proof serves to speed up your proof, make your claim easier to grasp and believe, and enable your prospects to remember it longer.

Claim Prover 4: Let Prospects Experience It Themselves

"The proof of the pudding is in the eating" is a time-proven adage. If you claim that your product is lightweight, let your prospect pick it up and carry it around. If you claim your product is simple and easy to use, let your prospect use it.

Claim Prover 5: Repeat Important Claims and Proofs Again and Again

Have you ever wondered why major companies keep repeating the *same*

> **Try It, You'll Like It!**
> This can be a tough assignment with some intangible products or personal services and with some types of selling, such as pure tele-sales. That's one reason why you may want to make "free trial offers." However, no matter how tough it is, every bit of creative effort you put into helping people experience for themselves the claims you make will be richly rewarded by an increase in your credibility.

commercials over and over? The truth is that a typical company may spend more money on air time to run a commercial just once than it spends actually making the product.

The reason companies keep repeating the same commercials over and over ad infinitum (sometimes ad nauseam) is that studies show it's the best way to get people to believe them, remember them, and act upon them.

When you're selling, the more often you repeat something, the better your chances that the prospect will accept it and remember it. That brings us to the second big task you have in the Convince step.

Bring Your Own Witnesses

What do the courts view as the strongest evidence in a trial? You guessed it—an eyewitness! What is the strongest theme in advertising? Word of mouth! Likewise, what's the most convincing evidence you can use to prove your claims for your product or service? An endorsement from a satisfied customer!

Here's a principle that explains why an endorsement is such powerful evidence that your product and service claims are true:

Convince Principle 3: Prospects expect salespeople to make claims for what they are selling, but they are impressed when someone else makes or endorses those claims.

So, never make a claim for yourself or your product that you can get someone else to make for you. Now, let's take a look at how you can use the powerful technique of bringing your own witnesses to effectively boost your sales.

Witness Pointer 1: Try to Get a Written Endorsement from Every Customer

The best way to get endorsements is to ask for them. It's that simple! Yet you'd be surprised at how many salespeople either neglect it or are afraid to do it.

Explain to your customers that their names are widely respected and that you would appreciate an opportunity to mention them as satisfied customers. Don't be surprised if, at this point, many of them will volunteer to write a letter for you. If they agree to allow you to use their name but don't actively volunteer to write a letter, come right out and ask for one. Only a very few will turn you down, usually for personal or professional reasons. From my experience, most people feel flattered that I think a letter from them will matter that much.

To make sure you get the promised letter, suggest coming by a few days later to pick it up and save the customer the trouble of mailing it. When you go back, always try to see your customer and thank him or her personally. Interestingly, you'll be surprised how many referrals you'll pick up on those second trips around.

One caution: make sure your satisfied customers understand that you plan to use their letters as a promotional device. If you don't and they find out you've used the letters, it can cause a misunderstanding.

> ### The Sales Machine
> **TRICKS OF THE TRADE**
>
> Kevin is vice president of sales for a national sales organization. He really got his sales people ahead of the game. He required each of them to provide three letters per month from satisfied customers. With 400 salespeople, that was 1200 letters per month!
>
> But he didn't stop there. He had the letters posted on his company's intranet, by customer type, so every salesperson in his organization could retrieve them easily—more than 7,000 letters a year from which to pick.
>
> Could you do the same thing? It's just a matter of your initiative.

Witness Pointer 2: Select Carefully the Endorsements You Use with Each Prospect

Let's face it: we're all imitators. We imitate the people we respect and admire and sometimes those we wish to impress. It's one of the strongest buying motivations.

Car dealers have made a very interesting discovery by asking people a few questions when they buy a new car. One of the most frequent reasons people give for buying a new car goes something like this: "My neighbor (or co-worker or friend) bought a new car, and I started thinking maybe it was time I looked into it."

Haven't you tried out a new restaurant or store or product because a friend said he or she liked it? Of course you have and so have I.

The more recognizable a name is, the more convincing it will be to your prospect. That's one good reason to find out during the Investigate and Probe steps all you can about every prospect you call on. If you can show a prospect an endorsement from a golfing or bridge partner, a business associate, or a personal friend, it's like money in the bank.

If you can't find an endorsement from someone the prospect knows, you might choose endorsements from people of similar ages, with similar interests, and of similar social status.

Witness Pointer 3: Treat Endorsements with Dignity and Respect

An endorsement letter is worth many times its weight in pure gold, so treat it with dignity and respect. That suggests several things.

First, always speak of your customers as if you think they are the greatest people in the world. They are!

Second, protect your endorsements. I would suggest you put them in plastic sleeves to keep them looking fresh and new.

Third, show your endorsements as if you feel you are granting the prospect a special privilege to see them. If, for example, you rapidly flip them across a table at a prospect, you create several problems:

- You don't give your client time to read them, so it appears as if you are hiding something.
- Your behavior is contemptuous of both the prospect and the folks who gave you an endorsement.
- You make the prospect hesitant to give you an endorsement. Who wants to be included in an arsenal of missiles you toss across tables at people?

People who give you endorsements show a great deal of trust and prospects watch the respect you give your customers. So treat them with dignity and respect.

Witness Pointer 4: Try to Involve Happy Customers with Prospects

Sometimes you can get a prospect to make an appointment for you with a friend, a neighbor, or an associate. If so, it's a most convincing piece of evidence.

What I'm talking about is vastly different from the old high-pressure tactic of giving people a discount or premium for furnishing you with leads or actually setting up appointments for you. Most people react very negatively to that sort of tactic.

Let me explain what I'm talking about by using the case of a furniture rep who works out of my area. This guy has set up a mutual sharing network among the dealers who buy from him. When a furniture retailer gets a big response from an ad or a sale on his products, the salesman will ask for permission to share that ad with other retailers in his territory but not in the same town. Since the salesman often shares winning ads and sales from other stores with him, he's usually glad to cooperate.

The salesman then takes that ad to other stores and suggests they run a similar sale—featuring his products, of course. "If you have any question about how well the ad works, call Joe at Smith's Furniture and ask him," he'll say. Sometimes he even suggests they call him "right now." If they call, Joe is proud of his idea and sells the prospect on it, the prospect is happy to find something that will sell furniture for him or her, and the salesman writes up a big order. That salesman has sold as much as five boxcar loads of furniture in one week, on one ad.

It takes a lot of creativity and some finesse to pull it off, but it is incredibly convincing. Why not look for some ways you can get your satisfied customers involved in selling for you?

Justify Your Price

We have already discussed justifying price in Chapter 9, as part of the Apply step. To repeat the best single piece of advice, "When presenting your price, you'll always want to present it within the structure of benefits." In other words, you justify your price before you even mention it.

Then, when you present the price, you should "stack" it between the benefits and the perceived emotional costs, so your prospect understands the price within the proper context.

If he or she tries to question the price by making comparisons to competing products or services, I advise the "apples and pears" strategy mentioned in Chapter 9. If you present your offering as distinct from any other offering on the market, you make it difficult or even impossible for a prospect to force you into defending your price.

Relieve Your Prospect's Fear of Buying

Fear can be one of the strongest motivations a prospect may have for buying a product or service, but it can also be one of the greatest deterrents to deciding positively.

In fact, fear of buying often proves to be one of the toughest challenges a salesperson faces. It may grow out of a fear of failure, a fear of poverty, a fear of ridicule or rejection, a fear of the unknown, and so on down a long list of possible fears.

Your task is to help prospects overcome enough of whatever fear they feel to make them comfortable enough to buy. How can you do that?

First, we'll look at an important principle of convincing your prospect. Then we'll explore some techniques you can use to make it work for you.

Convince Principle 4: As trust in you and confidence in the value you are offering rises, fear of buying disappears.

The greatest fear busters are trust and value. Let's look at some ways you can make them work for you as you seek to convince your prospects to buy.

Buying Fear Reliever 1: Reconcile the Buying Decision with Their Value System

Any time we set out to act in a manner that is inconsistent with the way we see ourselves, we can expect to feel some fear. That's true even if what we are doing is a very good thing.

For example, many people who leave a "secure" job with a steady salary to work in sales on straight commission are scared that they will fail and be humiliated. Years from now, they may look back on it as one of the greatest steps they ever took, but for the moment it is threatening to their value system.

That same sort of dynamic often shows up when a person starts to buy something—especially if it costs a great deal or if it represents a significant change in their lives.

Persons who have been renting for years, for example, may feel as if they are taking on the national debt when they sign a mortgage contract for a house. That buying decision may be a very sound one for them, but it will feel like a violation of the values they have lived by for so long.

One of the real services you as a professional can render is to help them reconcile their choice with their value system. Thus, it is often helpful to explore very openly the fears they are feeling so they can become aware of their value system and its limitations.

Buying Fear Reliever 2: Help Them Expand Their Own Self-Belief

All of us have our own self-belief system—that imaginary world inside of which we feel safe, comfortable, and satisfied. Any time we start to do something that violates that world, we feel that we are on dangerous ground. As a result, we become afraid to try things that our emotions have not allowed us to experience before.

You can help your prospects overcome such fears by enabling them to reevaluate their self-belief systems. One way to do that is to help them focus on how great the benefits of ownership will make them feel. Another way is to help them gradually experience what ownership will be like.

Buying Fear Reliever 3: Assure Them of the Wisdom of Their Choices

Some people may be so self-confident that they don't feel hesitant to buy anything they want or need. However, those people are few and far between. For most people, buying is an unsettling experience.

A thousand questions may be rushing through a prospect's mind as he or she contemplates a decision to buy: Is this the right thing for me to do? What will so-and-so think about my decision? Can I pay for this thing? Is it really me? Do I really need it?

You can do prospects a big favor, and boost your chances for closing a sale, by reassuring them of the wisdom of their decision. Of course you can't tell them they are doing the right thing, any more than you can tell them that not buying is the wrong thing for them to do. You are not a judge and you don't have to be. What you can do, however, is reassure them that they are making a wise decision—at least from a values perspective. Here are some ways you can do that.

First, you have to believe it yourself. That's one reason I'd have a hard time selling certain things to some people. For instance, I'd have a hard time selling expensive jewelry to someone whose children wore shabby shoes. If you know in your heart that a decision is not wise for a person, you are not much of a professional if you try to convince him or her otherwise. But if you know it's a wise decision, then reassure your prospect with all your persuasive power.

Second, recap the benefits to show how wise the decision is. You'll be amazed at how often a major benefit dawns on a prospect only the fifth or sixth time you repeat it. Don't assume he or she understands each benefit; make sure.

Third, reinforce all the prospect's positive feelings about buying. If a prospect expresses a liking for some benefit, get him or her to talk more about it. If a prospect is silent, ask what he or she likes most about what you've shown. Give your prospect an opportunity to take psychological possession by asking what he or she is looking forward to the most. The more the prospects are talking positively about the benefits you've shown, the more they are selling themselves.

Fourth, answer any questions your prospects may have. Honesty is the best policy throughout the sales process, but both honesty and complete openness are necessary during the Convince step. Stop everything you are doing and ask if they have any questions they'd like to ask. Now is the time to find out if there are objections and what they are. In the next step, I'll share some insights on how to handle objections. But one thing you certainly never do is take them lightly. Deal with them as they come up or they will act like earmuffs to block out everything you say.

One caution: if you ask for questions, then appear to hedge on an answer, that can destroy all the convincing you've done during this all-important step.

Checklist for Chapter 10

❑ There are some salespeople whose lack of credibility hurts a lot of other salespeople. Polls often place salespeople very low in terms of believability or honesty.

❑ If people believe strongly enough that what you are selling will be worth more to them than the money you're asking for it, they'll buy it, and if they don't, they won't! It's that simple.

❑ To make a great living at selling, you must find ways to cut through all the mistrust and conflicting values to convince your prospects that what you say is true and that the benefits outweigh the price.

❑ There are four actions you can take in the Convince step to set the stage for your prospects to buy:
1. Prove your claims.
2. Bring your own witnesses.
3. Justify your price.
4. Relieve the prospects' fear of buying.

❑ Most prospects will not believe anything you say unless you prove it to them. There are five ways to prove every claim about your product or service, your company, and yourself:
1. Never make a claim you can't back up with facts.
2. If you can prove it, show your evidence.
3. Reinforce all claims visually.
4. Let prospects experience it themselves.
5. Repeat important claims and proofs again and again.

❑ Prospects expect salespeople to make claims, but they are impressed when someone else makes or endorses those claims. Here are four ways to bring witnesses to your prospect:
1. Try to get a written endorsement from every customer.
2. Select carefully the endorsements you use with each prospect.
3. Treat endorsements with dignity and respect.
4. Try to involve happy customers with prospects.

❑ Fear can be one of the strongest motivations prospects may have for buying, but it can also be one of the greatest deterrents. Here are three ways to relieve your prospects' fear of buying:

1. Reconcile the buying decision with their value system.
2. Help them expand their own self-belief.
3. Assure them of the wisdom of their choices.

The Tie-It-Up Step: Concluding and Closing

Tie it up: Asking the prospect to buy, negotiating agreement, finalizing, reinforcing, and then cementing the sale. It is through servicing your new customer in ways that guarantee more sales, strong referrals, and an ongoing, productive relationship.

Tie up the Sale, Not the Customer

Closing a sale is not using clever gimmicks to trick people into something they really don't want to do. Closing is not the centerpiece of a sale, around which all other elements are built. Rather, tying up the sale is the natural outgrowth of doing the other five steps well. It's an orderly and simple step taken deliberately at the end of a series of steps. It can be fun—both for you and for the prospect.

Remember: people want what you're selling or they wouldn't buy it. In fact, they probably wanted it before you even entered the scene. Perhaps they didn't know they wanted it until you showed them what they really wanted, or maybe you did such a good job that you made them want your particular brand, model, or option. At any rate, you cannot build a successful sales career by roping today's alert consumers and professional buyers into buying things they really don't want.

So, if they want it and you want to sell it, then it's a simple process of tying up the loose ends of the transaction. As with each of the steps, there are certain tested and proven procedures you can follow.

Negotiate the Conditions of the Sale

Successful negotiating is working out an agreement that's mutually satisfactory for both or all parties to do something they both or all want to do. It's handling the details in a way that enables everybody to win.

In a way, everything you have done up to this point has been a part of negotiating the sale. If you've followed the IMPACT Selling System, you have already done the following:

1. Investigated to discover who was most interested in your business proposal.
2. Met with qualified prospects to enter into dialogue on your proposal.
3. Probed to find out what they wanted most and under what conditions they would buy it.
4. Applied your most appropriate solution to their most compelling needs and desires.
5. Convinced them that you can solve their problems and fulfill their wishes by buying what you are selling.

That's the informal part of negotiating; without it you cannot enter into formal negotiations. If you skip over any one of those steps, it will sabotage even your best efforts to tie up the sale.

If you have, in fact, completed the first five steps, you are now ready to start the formal negotiating process. Here are some winning strategies to help you become an effective negotiator.

Open the Negotiations on a Positive Note

A great time to open up the formal negotiations is right after your prospect has expressed approval or delight over some feature or benefit. You simply ask, "Is there anything that would keep you from going ahead with this?" Then *stop!*

This simple question is the most useful question ever devised for opening up any negotiation. It's a sincere and honest question, it cuts right through to the heart of the matter, and it is not in any way offensive. But the key to asking it properly is to stop after you've asked it and wait for the prospect to respond.

The question says it all. Be sure to listen very carefully to what the prospect says. If he or she says, "No!" or "I don't see any reason not to go ahead," you can assume the sale and begin taking care of the details. Very often, however, the prospect will show some hesitancy and offer some reason for not going ahead. If so, don't panic. Just go to the next strategy. It, too, is very simple, clear, and easy to do.

Get All the Conditions and Objections on the Table

Prospects will almost never say, "I'll buy it under the following conditions." More often their response will take the form of "I don't know! That's a lot of money!" or "I wish you offered it in a different color." Expect this sort of response. Don't be shocked when it occurs, because it will. At this point, lots of salespeople react somewhat hysterically and start hammering away at all the reasons why the price or another issue shouldn't make a difference. And that's a big mistake!

It's a mistake because most stated conditions are only smokescreens to cover up deeper feelings of uncertainty. You simply cannot negotiate with a smokescreen—as soon as you satisfy one condition, the prospect will raise another.

Here's where you need to return to the Probe step, because the IMPACT Selling System is really a closed-loop system. When you meet resistance of any sort, you simply return to the Probe. That's the only way you can get all the conditions on the

Is It the Size?

Andrea was sure she'd presented the best option for her diagnostic imaging equipment to Dr. Jones. She had asked the right questions, presented the equipment in the correct manner, and provided the names of five other radiologists who had been using the equipment successfully for years.

She asked Jones, "Is there anything that would keep you from going ahead?" His response was a simple, "Yes." She was calm, cool, and in control. She then asked, "What is it that would keep you from purchasing the equipment?" He answered, "I'm not sure if it will fit where I need it to go. My office is awfully small."

Andrea then asked, "Is there anything other than the space issue that would cause you not to go ahead?" He assured her that if it could fit, she had a deal.

Where did Andrea make her mistake? How can she recover?

She handled and isolated the objection very well. Now, the single issue is whether she can convince her prospect that the equipment will fit—or find a better place to put it!

negotiating table so you can deal with them. Ask questions such as "Is this the only reason you'd be hesitant to go ahead?" or "If I could show you how to solve that problem, could I presume you'd be ready to go ahead?" By pursuing this line of questioning you'll eventually bring all conditions of purchase into the open.

Don't be afraid of this process. It's better to have negative feelings and thoughts come out at this stage. Once you feel you have all the conditions on the table, you can proceed to the next strategy.

Make Sure You Understand All the Conditions

Often, you'll discover that there is more than one reason why someone is hesitant to buy. In order to uncover them, remember, you will have asked, "Is that the only reason you'd be hesitant to go ahead?"

Make sure you understand the conditions your prospect has listed. If there are several reasons, a good thing to do is to make a list of them and read them off to your prospect. Restate them in your own words and ask if you have really understood what he or she is feeling.

"OK," you might say, "let me see if I understand what you've told me. You feel uncertain that you can handle an expenditure of this size right now and you would prefer a different color and size. Is that right?"

It's important that you clearly understand exactly what the prospect feels and demands. It's equally important that the prospect understands that you know what he or she feels. The only way you can reach that kind of understanding is through dialogue. For example, you may surmise that a prospect is feeling, "I can't afford this," but what the person's actually feeling may be "I can't justify spending that much money for this item." There is a big difference between those two positions. Stay with the dialogue process until you are confident that you and the prospect agree on what the stated conditions mean.

> ### It's More Than the Size
> What if Andrea had asked, "Is there anything that would keep you from going ahead?" and the doctor had answered, "Yes," but then she either failed to ask what the issue was ("space") or, worse yet, didn't ask if there were other issues to consider? What if it was also delivery times? How about warranty questions, terms, or training on the equipment?
>
> You need to uncover every issue that's a stumbling block to the sale and deal with them. Every one!

Offer to Try to Work out Any Problems

At this point, you want to make it clear to your prospect that both of you are sitting on the same side of the negotiating table. In effect, you're saying, "I know you'd like to have the benefits I've shown you, but I do know you have some concerns. I want to help you deal with those concerns so you can enjoy the value of our product and the benefits you want." To do this, you'll simply agree with your prospect and offer to help him or her work out any problem.

The important thing is that you come out of the first strategy with a clear understanding of every single condition under which your prospect will buy and a continuing trust between you and the prospect that you're interested in providing exactly what he or she wants.

Clear Away Objections

Objections are the remaining conditions that you must deal with before a sale can be consummated. The way you handle objections will often determine whether or not you make the sale.

Almost always, a prospect will raise an objection from a feeling rather than a factual standpoint. Practically, this means you need to deal with all objections by addressing the actual feelings behind them. The salesperson who responds flippantly to a price objection by saying, "Sure it's a lot of money, but look what all you're getting!" is only asking for trouble.

The reason why most salespeople deal so poorly with objections is that they don't know how. All their training has focused on giving them canned responses to every objection that could possibly come up. They sound like a recorded message: "If prospect gives objection number four, you answer that with response number 67." And that approach is just plain wrong.

Simplify the Objection

At least half the work of solving any problem is to state that

It's All in the Question

Some salespeople will often rephrase an objection back to the prospect in the form of a question. For example, "What I hear you saying is that the color is not quite right. Is that correct?" or "What I understand you to mean is that you're not sure that the engine will handle the load. Is that right?"

That question helps the prospect clarify the objection in his or her own mind as well. It's not unusual for a prospect to hear the salesperson phrase the objection and realize that it really isn't as big an issue as he or she thought.

problem clearly and succinctly. In fact, when an objection is verbalized so that a prospect can really understand how he or she actually feels, it quite often disappears.

It's not always easy, but it always helps for you to know exactly what that prospect is feeling and for him or her, too, to know what he or she is feeling. That's what you achieve when you break an objection down to its simplest form and state it as a question.

Make Sure They Understand All the Benefits

It's wrong to assume a prospect understands all the benefits you've explained just because you've covered them several times. Make sure your prospect fully understands them. Go over and over them again and again.

Will and His Cabinets

Will learned this lesson the hard way. Will sold kitchen cabinetry. His products were durable, customizable, and easy to install. When he met with prospects, he would go down the list of benefits that his product provided his prospects.

When he lost a sale to his biggest competitor, he asked his former prospects why they had bought from his archrival. The answer confused him: "We really liked their cabinets' ease of installation." Will was shocked.

Whose fault was that? You guessed it: it was Will's fault. His prospects never really got the picture because he never made it clear enough. It was clear to Will, but not clear to the ones who counted the most—his prospects.

Test to See That the Objection Is Gone

Amateurs at selling brush aside objections with canned responses. After sweeping them under the rug, they proceed as if there were no conflicts in the prospect's mind. Then when they walk out without an order, they wonder why the person didn't buy.

By contrast, smart sales professionals always test to make sure that they've handled each objection to the prospect's satisfaction. They check to make sure it is gone and that it won't come back to haunt them.

After you've presented benefits, it's always smart to ask the prospect's reaction: "Does that answer your concern?"

It's a simple test, but it does two important things. First, it lets you know if the objection is gone. If it's still there, you can ask what concern the prospect still has and get more specific with it again, if necessary. Second, it provides an opportunity for the prospect to verbalize his or her own way of dealing with the objection. You'll be surprised how often prospects will pick right up on it. "Sure, I remember a drill I once bought that I first thought would wear out, but I used it for years and years."

Now you're ready for the next big step.

Ask for the Order

Everything you've done up to this point is wasted motion—unless you ask for the order. However, that's not as big a deal as many salespeople make it out to be. If you have carefully followed the first five steps—found out what your prospects want most, shown them how they can get it, and negotiated all the conditions necessary for the sale—asking for the order is a natural and logical step.

You can't make the buying decision for them, but you can facilitate the decision-making process for them. Let's look at some tested and proven techniques for making the buying decision easier for you and for your prospects.

Ask Them to Buy Now

When you feel the time is right, just come right out and ask for the order. However, the way you ask for an order can make it either easy or difficult for the prospect to make a buying decision.

Remember the early question: "Is there anything that would keep you from going ahead with this?" There was nothing tricky about it. You don't need tricks if you've done a good job of selling.

Asking for the order is merely a matter of tying up the loose ends of the sale. You look your prospect straight in the eye, ask him or her to buy, and then write! Don't say another word until your prospect has responded.

Many salespeople are so afraid of refusal that they feel they must break any silence that lasts more than a few seconds. They may even jump in and say something illogical like "Now I don't want to make you feel pressured" or "Maybe you want more time to think about this." All that does is delay the decision and perhaps permanently sabotage your effort. Try to remember that some people just need a little space when they're making a decision.

Since some people are reluctant to use such a direct close, let's look at two other strategies that also work well.

Assume the Sale

For many smart salespeople, it works better to simply assume that the prospect has bought and start handling the paperwork related to the sale, all the while asking the prospect questions about details.

When you finish the paperwork, you might ask, "Is there anything else we should discuss before we finalize the agreement?" If not, simply hand the prospect the order form, letter of agreement, or contract to sign.

The chief advantage to this approach is that prospects never have to make one big decision to buy, just a series of little decisions, and many prospects feel much more comfortable with that. The chief disadvantage is that some people may feel pressured if they are not quite ready to make a decision. If that happens, lay the paperwork aside and return to the Probe step to find out why they are hesitant.

The Alternative Strategy

Another way to make it easy for prospects to decide to buy is to give them a choice other than "yes" or "no." You can do this with the alternative strategy, sometimes known as the either/or close.

It works like this. You ask a question that lets them choose between having it one way or another: "Do you like it best in red or would you rather have the blue?" "Can I schedule delivery on Wednesday or do you prefer that I schedule it for next

Monday?" "Do you prefer to pay cash or would you rather use our payment plan?"

A way to lead into an either/or question is to summarize the benefits and restate the price just before you ask the question. Another good approach is to ask the question immediately after the prospect has made a positive statement about some feature or benefit he or she particularly likes.

The greatest advantage of the alternative strategy is that it shields people from ever having to make a buying decision as such. They simply choose the model they want or the conditions under which they will buy. It's probably the closing technique with which most prospects will feel the least pressure.

Deal with Fear of Making a Decision

Often you will find that a prospect is sold on your product and feels comfortable with all the conditions of the purchase, but is simply hesitant to make a buying decision.

Don't Rush the Prospect!

Paul sells mortgages. A prospect once stopped him and said, "Look! If you can give me a few minutes to think about this, I might say 'yes.' If you have to know right now, the answer is *no*!"

"Take as much time as you like!" Paul said, with a great big smile. He quickly laid the contract aside and he and his prospect talked for 20 minutes about her family. Then she signed the paperwork without a moment's hesitation.

If you sense that your prospect needs more than a little time or space to make a decision, it's a good idea to probe into exactly why he or she is hesitant. If you discover there's some key issue, try to settle it just as you would handle any objection and go on with the transaction.

Usually it helps to focus that key issue as precisely as possible by returning to the Probe step. You can do that by asking, "If it weren't for the balloon note at the end of the lease agreement, would you be ready to go ahead with this?"

If the prospect says "Yes," then you know exactly what you are dealing with and can try to negotiate a new set of conditions he or she could accept. If not, you need to keep probing until you pin down that one key factor and deal with it.

Reinforce and Cement the Sale

Once a prospect makes a decision to buy, many salespeople start packing up and getting out as fast as they can. They seem to feel they should evacuate the premises before the prospect changes his or her mind. That's a big mistake!

If customers want to back out, they'll find a way to back out—no matter what they've signed. What's more, your haste to get out of there can damage the trust bond you've worked so hard to create. It's better to take a few minutes to tie up some loose ends before you leave.

I recommend reinforcing the sale with any of several strategies.

Compliment Your New Customer on His or Her Choice

Saying, "I think you've made a great choice" is a simple yet very effective way to reinforce the sale. What makes it so helpful is

It's Not Just the Software

Lori sells accounting software to small and medium-sized businesses. She is very careful to be sure that she prescribes just the right software package to address each prospect's situation.

She then knows that the software her customers buy is 100% accurate for their situations.

Once she has made a sale, she then congratulates her new customer on having made exactly the right choice. But she goes even further and tells them why it's the perfect choice. It could be ease of use, simple-to-read spreadsheets, the variety of reports the software can generate, or the way it can categorize accounts. Whatever it is that made that product the exact right choice for her customer is what she stresses when she congratulates him or her for purchasing.

How can you do the same thing for your customers?

that it not only congratulates the customer on his or her purchase, but opens the door for him or her to express positive feelings about the purchase. The more the customer talks about it, the more comfortable he or she will become with the decision.

This self-acknowledgment can help to head off several problems. For example, if someone your customer respects questions his or her decision later, your customer will have become resolute enough in the decision that he or she is not likely to be talked out of it.

Invite Your Customer to Buy More

Very often the best prospect for a sale is the new customer to whom you've just sold your product or service.

Assure Your Customer of Satisfaction

It's a good idea to reassure your customers that they are not alone after the sale or dealing with strangers from some impersonal organization they can hardly make contact with. Just promise, "I'll check back with you next week to make sure you got everything OK." You might want to add, "If you have any problems with delivery, feel free to call me."

However, if you promise to check back with your customers, make sure you do. If there is a problem and you don't check back, you'll only compound the anger they feel.

It's All About Service

Now the hard part starts. You've made the sale and your new job is to deliver more than you even promised. Your job is to ensure that whatever you sold is delivered, serviced, and handled in precisely the way you promised that it would be. To do anything less is to abdicate your position as a sales professional. It also shortchanges your customer.

Don't be tempted to walk away and hope your customers will be happy. The only way to guarantee their satisfaction is for you to monitor the activity that goes on with their account.

But remember: there's good reason for that. Not only does it ensure that they've received what you've sold them, but it also

Why Sell One When You Can Sell Two?

Steve bought his first Mercedes several years ago. After giving the young salesperson a check for about $75,000 for a sedan, he stood in the lobby and chatted with the man and his sales manager.

The young fellow was evidently still in training, but it was the sales manager who seemed new: his anxiety was obvious as he kept trying to hurry Steve out the door.

"You've made a wise investment and I think you are in for a real treat when you discover what's so special about owning a Mercedes," the young salesperson said.

"Thanks," Steve replied. "I'm sure I'll enjoy it!"

"In fact," the salesperson mused, "there's only one way you can make a better decision than the one you've just made." At this, the sales manager rolled his eyes toward the ceiling as if to say, "What am I going to do with this kid!"

"How's that?" Steve asked.

"Go ahead and let me deliver that sports model we talked about for your wife, too!" he said with a grin.

Steve thought for a minute. "I'll tell you what. You find me a metallic gray with a blue top and you've just sold yourself another car!"

As he handed the salesperson a second check, Steve asked, "When was the last time you sold two cars, worth $150,000, in about 15 minutes?"

"Never!" came the reply immediately. That might very well have been because he'd never dared to ask anyone to buy a second car.

The moral of the story: you never know unless you ask. A person who is sold on a product might add on to the sale, might upgrade his or her choice, or might even duplicate it.

gives you the opportunity to sell them more and maximize your relationship for positive, productive referrals.

Here's the issue. Your job is to develop your new customers to the point that they're active advocates or zealots for you and your services. There's no better way to more sales and more raving fans for you, your products or services, and your organization.

Professional selling requires a lot of hard, diligent work. However, there's not a greater profession in the world. But if you can't finalize transactions, you'll never succeed at sales. It's all about transferring your product or service from your ownership to theirs. That's what sales is all about, isn't it?

Checklist for Chapter 11

❑ Successful negotiating is working out an agreement that's mutually satisfactory for both or all parties. It's handling the details in a way that enables everybody to win.

❑ A great time to open up the formal negotiations is right after your prospect has expressed approval or delight over some feature or benefit. Ask, "Is there anything that would keep you from going ahead with this?" Then *stop!*

❑ When you meet resistance of any sort, you simply return to the Probe step.

❑ Make it clear to your prospect that both of you are sitting on the same side of the negotiating table.

❑ Objections are the remaining conditions that you must deal with before a sale can be consummated. The way you handle objections will often determine whether or not you make the sale.

❑ Most salespeople deal so poorly with objections because all their training has focused on giving them canned responses to objections.

❑ Don't assume a prospect understands all the benefits you've explained. Make sure. Go over and over them again and again.

❑ Smart sales professionals always test to make sure that they've handled each objection to the prospect's satisfaction.

❑ When you feel the time is right, just come right out and ask for the order. However, the way you ask can make it either easy or difficult for the prospect.

❑ If you sense your prospect needs more than a little time or space to make a decision, probe into exactly why the prospect is hesitant. If you discover there is some key issue, try to settle it just as you would handle any objection and go on.

❏ After you make the sale, reinforce the sale. There are several strategies to build on the trust you've developed, to be supportive of your customer, and perhaps to sell more.

How to Build and Sustain Sales Momentum

We've discussed that success is what really breeds motivation, that it's extremely difficult to build and sustain legitimate motivation if you're experiencing failure after failure. However, why is it that some people seem to be consistently optimistic and enthusiastic about what they do no matter what the short-term outcome?

Motivation, Resilience, and Optimism

First, let's look at two other realities:

- You are responsible for your own motivation, resilience, and optimism.
- You are both responsible and accountable for your own sales results and performance.

Don't believe that it's someone else's responsibility to make you successful. It doesn't work that way. It's strictly and solely up to you to create your success. It's that simple.

Successful salespeople share some common traits:

- They have strong product knowledge that can be applied with 100% accuracy toward addressing a prospect's need or solving a prospect's problems.

> **Motivation** The drive to perform.
>
> **Resilience** The capacity to rebound from setbacks or difficulties.
>
> **Optimism** The belief that positive outcomes will be the result of your actions.

- They have strong selling skills that give them the confidence to perform at high levels of success.
- They have the capacity to be optimistic, resilient, and competitive in the face of any obstacle.
- They have the physical stamina and resolution to work as long and as hard as necessary to succeed.
- They enjoy selling, take pleasure in seeing themselves in the role of sales professionals, and are fueled by the rewards that the profession of sales gives them.

The 10 Most Essential Success Truths in Professional Selling

There is no doubt about it. All success in sales starts on the inside. In order to help get you started, let's take a look at the 10 most essential success truths that are critical to your sales success.

1. Success is progressive and gradual. It's never a one-time, cataclysmic event.

Your sales success will occur over time. Don't rely on one big sale or one prospect to propel you to your organization's sales hall of fame. Instead, realize that long-term success is far more a function of working to your fullest capacity day after day. It's a series of victories that, over time, will contribute to taking you to whatever success you seek.

2. Life isn't fair. Nobody starts out equal with anyone else. So get over it and move on.

Sprint to the Line

Sales success is not a marathon race. Instead, it's a long-term series of sprints that you'll run one at a time.

Top salespeople tend to win smaller victories more often. They're not people who have long droughts between victories. If they have a big win, they celebrate it and quickly move on to another challenge, no matter the size.

Stop comparing yourself with someone else. Why is that? Because you're not someone else. You are you—and not one other person on earth has your exact DNA, skills, or background. As a consequence, it's impossible for people to be on equal footing.

Start comparing yourself with your own potential. What does that mean? Great salespeople don't compare themselves with other salespeople. They don't wish they had a better territory or set of customers. Instead, they dig in and make themselves responsible for maximizing every opportunity that comes their way.

Life Can Be a Total Funk

Brad always seemed depressed. He would have an occasional selling success and would then slip into a funk that lasted for weeks. He couldn't believe that Rosemary, the boss's daughter, kept getting more territory. He also was upset by the sales contests that always seemed to favor his friend, Matt, whose customers always bought the products that earned the most points for sales contests. Matt had apparently inherited the territory from his uncle John, who had retired. He even believed that the sales manager was stacking the contests so that Rosemary would win.

What was Brad's problem? Was he jealous of Rosemary and Matt? Even if he was, what good did it do him? What could he do about it? Could he work harder to sell more and help himself win more of the sales contests?

3. Self-discipline is the universal differentiator between highly successful and marginally successful people.

The most successful salespeople are the most disciplined. There's not a profession in the world that looks like it requires

Who's Cheating Whom?

Cindy was in sales. However, she also had a part-time business. Because her job allowed her the freedom to come and go as she pleased, she was able to squeeze more and more of her business activities into the time that she was supposed to be spending selling for her employer.

Over time, she started to actually make sales calls for her business during regular office hours. She also started selling her sideline services to her employer's prospects. Her belief was that if she delivered acceptable results for her employer, all would be fine.

What do you think about her self-discipline? What problems is it causing? How honest is Cindy being? What would you do if you were her manager and discovered that she was doing this?

less discipline, yet actually requires more self-discipline than sales. It's tempting to be as free as a bird and spend all of your time doing the wrong things. Top salespeople stay on task … and they don't need any outside push to remind them that they should be prospecting, making face-to-face presentations, servicing accounts, or working on their career.

4. Successful people have unique and in-depth wisdom and insight about their area of endeavor that others don't have.

How much time, energy, effort, and commitment are you prepared to invest to be a top sales professional? Are

Where Will You Be in Two Years?

Smart salespeople devour every sales magazine, newsletter, audio program, or journal they can find. They become absolute masters of their craft. They buy books and audio programs, attend seminars or workshops, and talk with great salespeople to learn how they excel.

If you'll invest just minutes every day in product knowledge, marketplace research, learning selling skills, personal growth, and acquiring more insight about sales, you'll be a peerless expert within two years. If you don't do any of that, in two years you'll still be two years older—but your insight, knowledge, and understanding about your profession will be where it is today. Is that where you want to be in two years?

you willing to study, learn, and master the skills, mindsets, competencies, and talent requirements that can give you the edge you need?

People who are masters of their craft see unique, different patterns and relationships that others don't see. They see opportunities where others see just a sea of despair. They relate things that others see as being unrelated. Others seek them out as experts, including their prospects.

5. Potential is not something to invest in as a worthwhile endeavor, not saved for the future.

One of the worst things you can hear is "You have great potential." Why is that? If you're over 10 or 12 years old, it means that you have ability that you're not using.

Is This as Good as It Gets?

The worst thing that ever happened to Marvin is that he graduated from a prestigious Ivy League university. The tragedy to befall Ike is that he was an NFL superstar. Meagan's problem was that she made a pile of money in her first job out of school.

All three of these people suffer from the same problem: they had potential, used it, and never renewed it. Do you know someone like that? Some people dwell in the past, either regretting times they can never live again or feeling totally satisfied with the success they enjoyed earlier in life.

Then there's Brad, who showed great promise as a singer, but never wanted to practice. There's Karen, who scored 1500 on her SATs but chose not to attend a prestigious university because she worried that it would be too difficult. And there's Nancy, whose sales manager told her that she could easily be salesperson of the year if she would just work two more hours a day. Unfortunately, Brad never sang, Karen never went to college, and Nancy refused to work two extra hours a day.

Which group of people is worse? Those who displayed great potential and then never renewed it? Those who never used their potential? It makes no difference, really, because they're both in the same place—nowhere. How about you? Are you using your potential?

Potential is a renewable resource. As you access it, you can always go back to your inner source and get more. As you grow and expand, that resource constantly reinvents itself and takes on a new shape, direction, and life.

6. No one will ever be any more successful than they see themselves as being.

We've talked about your self-image earlier. However, it's something that bears being revisited.

Here's why. You will never achieve any level of meaningful success that flies in the face of the self-image that you've created for yourself. Unfortunately, that self-image is the cumulative result of everything you have ever understood as being said, written, or otherwise communicated about you. If what you've heard is real, your self-image will be strong. However, it doesn't take very much to pollute your mind—perhaps only a negative word here or there. Unfortunately, it takes a lot more than you'd ever imagine to repair even minimal damage.

You can only change your self-image over time. You'll need to develop a set of affirmations, visualize yourself being successful and then be about the business of making yourself successful.

Just an Occasional Discouraging Word

Barb's mother was a very caring and loving person. She generally affirmed Barb and did her best to enhance her self-worth and give her confidence. However, on numerous occasions, her mother confided in her that, as a child, she herself was awkward in delicate situations ... and that Barb would likely have the same problem. Every time an awkward situation would come up, she would remind Barb how she would likely not handle it as well as she should.

Just last week, Barb's boss asked her to handle a very delicate situation with an awkward billing error that had occurred with Barb's top customer. Barb didn't sleep for two nights and mentally rehearsed every word she'd use. And she still entered the scene nervous and lacking confidence.

Does this situation sound familiar? How do you think she handled it? If she handled it well, how easy was it for her?

7. Success is more often about listening than about talking.

We've discussed this concept a great deal throughout this book. However, it's certainly worth revisiting—it's that important. When you do all the talking, you are really explaining things you already know. When you listen to others, you'll learn what they know. And there's a big difference.

You will have a great deal more success in any venture in life, whether it's sales or not, if you'll learn to be more interested in other people, in learning about their ideas, philosophies, or point of view.

Think about this for just a moment. If I listen to you, I'll learn about you, your interests, your dislikes, your likes, and your preferences. If you listen to me and I do all the talking, I'll never learn any of those things.

MISTAKE PROOFING

Questions for You

Let me ask you a few questions:

- What have you enjoyed most about this book?
- Which principle or strategy have you found most applicable to your sales career?
- How will you put it into practice?
- How valuable would it be to you if we had a discussion and I told you what I enjoyed about the book, the strategy that I find most valuable, and how I will put it into practice?

When you ask other people their opinions, points of view, or perspectives, you learn a lot more than if you do all the talking. And success is all about learning, isn't it?

8. Don't major in minors or confuse activity with results. It is entirely possible to be extremely busy doing all the wrong things.

As a salesperson, time is your only inventory. You need to be 100%, absolutely positive that you're doing the right things at the right time for the right reasons.

In order to do that, you'll need to have a clarified focus on those things that are most essential for your success—carefully positioning yourself, prospecting, pre-call planning, being in front of qualified prospects, making effective presentations, servicing accounts, seeking referrals, or productively learning more about your marketplace, products, and professional selling.

It's All About Time

Sylvia has been selling interior landscaping services for over a year. Her organization supplies plants, trees, and design services for offices. Most of her prospects are professional offices and commercial real estate developers.

However, Sylvia is frustrated. Her sales performance is getting worse by the month. She's active in a women's softball league, is a part-time artist, tends to her horse that she rides on the weekends, and is trying to build her part-time network marketing career.

What advice would you offer Sylvia to help increase her sales?

9. Successful people master their emotions, instead of allowing their emotions to master them.

How good are you at "compartmentalizing" your life? How effective are you at preventing a setback or failure in one part of your life from spilling over into another area of your life?

Do you allow personal problems to affect your professional performance? Do you allow professional setbacks to affect your personal life?

If you allow either of these things to happen, you will never experience the success you deserve. Even a cursory look at life will tell you that the most successful people in any venture are able to move past difficulties, problems, or obstacles and don't allow these problems to distract or derail them from

A Great Way to Get into Trouble

Richard prided himself on his ability to close sales. In fact, his colleagues gave him a fitting name, "Bulldog."

However, Richard sometimes let his emotions get the best of him. He recently lost a sale to a competitor. Not being one to take something like that without a fight, he actually confronted the customer. He wanted to know why they didn't buy from him, how they could justify spending more money with his competitors, and what he had to do to get the business. He was obnoxious and pushy according to the customer—who called Richard's boss.

That escalated into a shouting match between Richard and his boss. Richard couldn't believe that his boss wouldn't side with him. After all, he was a great salesperson.

Emotions are important. They are part of who you are. However, if you allow anger, frustration, or any other emotionally charged attitude to override your good sense or judgment, you'll likely regret what you did for a long time to come.

10. Successful people have heroes. They then work hard to become someone else's hero.

Who is your hero? Who is your role model? If you don't have one, find one. Ask yourself how that person would handle the difficulties, frustrations, and challenges you face in your sales career. Then model his or her behavior.

Here's your real challenge. Work hard to be someone else's hero. Use the ideas in this book and I guarantee you *will* become someone's hero, someone's sales hero. And then you really will have become successful, won't you?

Checklist for Chapter 12

❏ You are responsible for your own motivation, resilience, and optimism.

❏ You are both responsible and accountable for your own sales results and performance.

❏ Remember the common traits of successful salespeople:

- They have strong product knowledge that can be applied with 100% accuracy toward addressing a prospect's needs or solving a prospect's problems.
- They have strong selling skills that give them the confidence to perform at high levels of success.
- They have the capacity to be optimistic, resilient, and competitive in the face of any obstacle.
- They have the physical stamina and resolution to work as long and as hard as necessary to succeed.
- They enjoy selling, take pleasure in seeing themselves in the role of sales professionals, and are fueled by the rewards that the profession of sales gives them.

❑ Here are the 10 most essential success truths:

1. Success is progressive and gradual.
2. Life isn't fair.
3. Self-discipline is the universal differentiator between highly successful and marginally successful people.
4. Successful people have unique, in-depth wisdom and insight about their area of endeavor that others don't have.
5. Potential is not something to be invested in as a worthwhile endeavor or be saved.
6. No one will ever be any more successful than they see themselves as being.
7. Success is more often about listening than about talking.
8. Don't major in minors or confuse activity with results.
9. Successful people master their emotions, instead of allowing their emotions to master them.
10. Successful people have heroes.

Index